James Hamilton Fyfe

Enterprise Beyond the Seas

Or, how great colonies were founded

James Hamilton Fyfe

Enterprise Beyond the Seas
Or, how great colonies were founded

ISBN/EAN: 9783744750998

Printed in Europe, USA, Canada, Australia, Japan

Cover: Foto ©ninafisch / pixelio.de

More available books at **www.hansebooks.com**

ENTERPRISE BEYOND THE SEAS;

OR,

HOW GREAT COLONIES WERE FOUNDED.

BY

J. HAMILTON FYFE,
AUTHOR OF "TRIUMPHS OF INVENTION AND DISCOVERY."

LONDON:
T. NELSON AND SONS, PATERNOSTER ROW;
EDINBURGH; AND NEW YORK.

1874.

Preface.

"IN the history of the world," says Bancroft, "many pages are devoted to commemorate the men who have besieged cities, subdued provinces, or overthrown empires: in the eye of reason and of truth, a colony is a better offering than a victory." In no field of enterprise have the courage, perseverance, and humanity of our countrymen been more conspicuously or honourably displayed than in the planting and rearing of our colonies. It has been said that the Anglo-Saxon race has a peculiar aptitude for the work of colonization; and, certainly, the success with which it has accommodated itself to changes of climate, gained the confidence and attachment of the natives, and developed the resources of virgin lands, confirms the idea. The behaviour of our countrymen towards the aborigines of the various countries in which they have settled has not been free from cruelty and deceit; but, on the whole, we must admit that it redounds to their credit, especially when we reflect on the provocations which they received, and the liability to misconception on both sides. Our first attempts at colonization were accompanied by the most formidable difficulties and the most overwhelming disasters; but the brave and steadfast spirit of the "planters" did not quail before accumulated calamities. "The ice," said one true-hearted Englishman struggling in a frail bark through a sea of crashing icebergs—"the ice is strong, but God is stronger." Such was the mood in which the early settlers faced their work. Famine, pestilence, raging elements, treacherous savages, and jealous rivals were strong to harass and destroy; but the Lord their God, in whom they had in their rough wayward hearts an intensely earnest and practical faith, was stronger still to deliver them from evil, and to crown with success those enterprises which they had undertaken,—not from a mere lust of gold, but in no mean measure for the glory of His name and the advancement of His kingdom among the heathen. Nor did they trust in vain. There were few of the pioneers of that great plantation work who could not match Increase Mather's "Catalogue of Remarkable Providences," in the story of their own eventful lives.

This little volume is not a systematic history. It is merely a series of sketches, intended to illustrate

British colonization in some of its social and romantic aspects. It does not trench on questions of politics or economy,—it avoids statistics. It does not treat of all of our colonies. It traces the career only of those which bear a sort of representative character, and only up to the point when the growing plantation subsides into a <u>settled province</u>. The events herein recorded are deeply interesting in themselves, and become still more so when they are connected with the prosperity of our empire and the spread of civilization and Christianity. They also possess another interest for the reflective reader. It has been remarked that it is a peculiarity of a great and conquering people, that they find themselves at the same time, though in different regions, in all the various stages through which societies must pass between their birth and their destruction. Thus, in Vancouver's Island and Columbia the British race may be said to be in vigorous infancy; in Australia, in early youth; in Canada, in all the vigour of manhood; in the United States, energetic, progressive, triumphant; and in Great Britain, in robust middle age. A general survey of our colonial annals may thus be as useful as a course of universal history, and may serve to illustrate, in a striking manner, the causes of the stability or decay of commonwealths.

J. H. F.

Contents.

THE FIRST ENGLISH COLONY—
    1. Sir Humphrey Gilbert, ... 11
    2. The Voyage of the *Golden Hind*, ... 19

THE FOUNDATION OF VIRGINIA—
    1. Roanoke, ... 31
    2. Captain John Smith, ... 39
    3. Sunshine and Shade, ... 57

THE COLONIZATION OF NEW ENGLAND—
    1. The Pilgrim Fathers, ... 69
    2. New Plymouth, ... 75
    3. Massachusetts, ... 84
    4. The English and the Indians, ... 89

PENN AND PENNSYLVANIA, ... 97

THE SCOTTISH COLONY OF DARIEN—
    1. William Paterson, ... 115
    2. The First Expedition, ... 120
    3. The Disasters at Darien, ... 125

DOMINION OF CANADA—
    1. Canada, ... 137
    2. Rupert's Land and the Red River Territory, ... 144
    3. Vancouver's Island and British Columbia, ... 147

THE AUSTRALIAN CONTINENT—
    1. Botany Bay, ... 157
    2. The Australian Pastures, ... 166
    3. The Gold Diggings, ... 176
    4. The Australian Interior, ... 185

THE BRITAIN OF THE SOUTH—
    1. The Islands of New Zealand, ... 203
    2. Progress of the Colony, ... 208

THE CAPE AND SOUTH AFRICA—
    1. The Boers, ... 217
    2. The False Prophet of the Kaffirs, ... 223

PITCAIRN'S ISLAND, ... 233

APPENDIX, ... 243

The First English Colony.

I.—SIR HUMPHREY GILBERT.
II.—THE VOYAGE OF THE *GOLDEN HIND*.

The First English Colony.

I.—SIR HUMPHREY GILBERT.

IT was in the stirring days of Queen Elizabeth that England first engaged in what Bacon calls the "ancient and heroical work of plantation." The reign of the Virgin Monarch was just one of those epochs when the old limits of thought and habitation begin to appear narrow and confined, and when men long to overleap and range beyond them. Under the noontide blaze of the "new light" of the Reformers, the old religion had become but "darkness visible." The firmament, which before had seemed but a flat canopy above the earth, had sunk back into a region of boundless space. A whole hemisphere had been discovered in the west. A new heaven and a new earth, as it were, had been brought within human ken. All old notions were upset, all old routine was broken through; and at the same time that fresh fields of speculation and enterprise were thrown invitingly open, the ancient standing-ground gave way, and the accustomed occupations fell into decline. Feudalism had been overthrown. The feudal lords no longer required to maintain an army of retainers. The abbeys no longer yielded support to a legion of monks and mendicants. In spite of legislative prohibition, the great sheep-farms were spreading over the country, swallowing up even villages and hamlets, and depriving the rustic population of its accustomed means of support. Agriculture was therefore declining. Manufactures had scarcely begun to occupy the people. England was at peace; a standing army had not yet been invented; and continental campaigns offered but a scant outlet for the hot-bloods of the nation. With employment languishing, and population increasing, men were falling into crime from sheer want of work: "Witness," says Hakluyt, "twenty tall fellows hanged last Rochester assizes for small robberies." Thus everything conspired to give an impulse to the search for occupation abroad. The direction of the search was determined by the magnetic attraction of gold. Europe was still ringing with the brilliant successes of the Spaniards, who, in seventeen short years, had overrun territories of immense extent, inhabited by numerous nations under regular governments, and teeming, not only with the most luxuriant vegetation, but with the most precious metals. Nothing was talked of among the active and daring spirits of the time but the riches and beauty of that new world, which was a Paradise above ground and an Ophir below. Reports were continually arriving of the discovery of new lands and nations, and the opening of virgin mines of wealth. These things, we know, did not lack embellishment in the tales of travellers; but there was so large a proportion of proved and acknowledged truth in all the falsehoods that were coined, that people at home found it difficult to separate fact from fiction, and invested those distant regions with all the marvels of fairy-land. Sceptics might shake their heads over stories of trees that bore gems for fruit, birds that laid golden eggs, and sheep that wore a golden fleece, fountains of perpetual youth, and hordes of Amazons; but the multitude lent them an eager and confiding ear, and even men of learning and travel were beguiled by some of them. Indeed, down to the last century many believed the legend of the golden city of Manoa, where Indians, decked with strings of pearls, and powdered from head to foot with shining gold dust, disported in pleasure-gardens full of "all kinds of herbs, flowers, and trees, of gold and silver." All this inflamed alike the curiosity and cupidity of Europe. The combined romance and profit of a voyage Westward, ho! were irresistible to men of every class. The scholar deserted his university, the courtier forsook the presence-chamber, the lawyer abandoned his files and parchments, while the chemist threw aside his crucibles, and owned that the true philosopher's stone was the compass which led him to the great western continent. Every adventurer flattered himself with the hope of bestowing his name upon a new land of promise, over which he would rule as viceroy; or, at least, of gaining fame and fortune at a stroke by the capture of a huge Spanish carrack bursting with precious plate.

The thirst for gold was, undoubtedly, the great agent in promoting voyages of discovery, and in preparing the way for colonization. Just as the search for the philosopher's stone and the *elixir vitæ* led the alchemists to the discovery of important principles in chemistry and medicine, so did the pursuit of El Dorado conduct adventurers to the great work of "plantation." But while the multitude was intent upon the glittering bait, there were not wanting men who had truer and nobler conceptions of the mission to be achieved in that wonderful new world, and who, in their earnest philanthropy, saw in the possession of a virgin land the means, not only of providing an outlet for our surplus population, but of conveying to the natives the benefits of civilization and the consolations of Christianity.

In the early days of Elizabeth's reign there stood an old manor-house at Greenaway, on a narrow tongue of land shooting out into the deep waters of the River Dart, in which one might have often seen, engaged in earnest conference on this great subject, a knot of men, destined to become not the least brilliant stars in that galaxy of noble spirits which illustrated the age, and which still glows on the field of history like the Milky Way in the heavens. One can fancy the group. There is Walter Raleigh, whose lofty forehead, piercing eye, and resolute mouth, remove the suspicion of foppery which his rich fantastic dress is apt to excite. Young in years, he has already given a foretaste of that power and versatility of mind, that force of character which afterwards made him one of the most eminent and many-sided men of his period,—soldier, sailor, scholar, courtier, orator, poet, philosopher, explorer of new lands and founder of new states. Beside him is his elder and half-brother, Humphrey Gilbert, whose serene and open countenance, bright kindly eye, and sanguine temperament, reveal the pure, unselfish, high-minded spirit of the man whose whole life was spent for the good of others, and formed the best commentary on his own noble saying: "Never mislike with me for taking in hand any laudable and honest enterprise; for if through pleasure or idleness we purchase shame, the pleasure vanisheth, but the shame abideth for ever: give me leave, therefore, without offence, always to live and die in this mind; for that he is not worthy to live at all that, for fear or danger of death, shunneth his country's service and his own honour, seeing that death is inevitable, and the fame of virtue immortal, wherefore in this behalf, *mutare vel timere sperno.*" There is Adrian Gilbert, too, full of faith in his elder brother Humphrey; and Richard

Grenville, fiery and valorous, — readier with his hand than his head to aid the scheme his friends have at heart. Over in France, and in the Low Countries, where he has been fighting for the Protestants, Raleigh has heard many a dark tale concerning the atrocities of the Spaniards in the fair new world, on which they had alighted as a curse;—how De Soto and his men, going up into a mountain to pray, suddenly came down, in sheer wanton thirst for blood, to hack and slay the unoffending, helpless Indians; how a Franciscan monk, who was with another expedition, with his own eyes saw above forty thousand natives perish by the edge of the sword, or in the fangs of savage dogs; how there were regions where you might journey for days with trees around you heavy with the bodies of Indians who had hanged themselves, in families and tribes, to escape the unspeakable cruelties of the invaders. One can fancy Raleigh recounting such things, and breaking forth into the exclamation which afterwards found its place among the "Incitements" to the Guinea colony: "If the Castilians, pretending a religious care of planting Christianity in those parts, have in their doings preached nought else than avarice, rapine, blood, death and destruction to those naked and sheep-like creatures of God, erecting statues and trophies of victory unto themselves in the slaughter of millions of innocents, doth not the cry of the poor succourless ascend unto the heavens?

Truly we have a work in this place,—instead of Papistry, to make the sincere light of the gospel to shine on this people." On many a weary march, on many a night-long watch by the flickering campfire, Raleigh, and his clever, "over-voluble" friend, Colonel Bingham, had debated the prospects of a plantation in America. Humphrey Gilbert, too, had had his thoughts on the matter. Led by the associations of his childhood to be fond of a sea life, he had mastered the science of navigation, scientifically and practically, and had been seized with a desire to take part in one of those voyages of exploration for which Elizabeth's reign is famous. With worthy Master Purchas he was moved to think there was "one thing yet left undone whereby a great mind might become notable;" and that was, the discovery of the North-west Passage to Cathay. His design, however, went beyond the mere discovery and nominal possession of a new land. He made the search for Meta Incognita secondary to the planting of a colony on the northern shores of America. Raleigh eagerly supported the scheme.

There was no difficulty in getting the sanction of the Crown to the enterprise. Sir Humphrey Gilbert was a favourite with the Queen, who had watched his career with interest from boyhood, and had given him to wife, as a special token of regard, one of her own maids of honour. Raleigh had not yet had the opportunity of flinging his cloak upon the muddy footway, but his name was known with credit out of court.

It was in 1578 that Sir Humphrey obtained from the Queen a grant of any "remote heathen or barbarous lands, not being actually possessed by any Christian prince or people," which he might discover. There had already been some talk of making a settlement in Newfoundland. When Frobisher made his second voyage to the fabled gold-mines of Hudson's Strait, he carried with him a number of men, who undertook to form a colony in that frozen and forbidding region; but when they reached the spot, the hardships they endured, and the immense quantity of black ore, supposed to contain the precious metal, enough "to suffice all the gold gluttons of the world," which they collected, rendered them anxious to return to England. The plan of a settlement was therefore abandoned, and the adventurers brought home their cargoes of worthless stones, concerning the destination of which no record survives. Sir Humphrey Gilbert, warned probably by the results of this expedition, gave little heed to the dazzling prospect of gold-fields in the ice-bound north. He saw a surer and richer mine of wealth in the shoals of cod-fish with which the waters of Newfoundland swarmed. Already four hundred vessels came annually from Spain, Portugal, France, and England to those teeming banks. The English were represented only by some thirty or forty sail; but they were "commonly lords of the harbours wherein they fished," receiving a tribute of fish and salt from the other vessels, as a return for their protection against the pirates who infested the coast. The title to the land was claimed by England, on the ground that it was discovered by the Cabots in 1497. Thither Sir Humphrey Gilbert resolved to transport his colony.

Many persons of good estate joined the expedition, and great preparations were made to insure its success. A strong fleet was got ready, "able to encounter a king's power by sea." But the enterprise did not thrive. Discord arose among the adventurers before they set sail, and a number deserted. Sir Humphrey had to put to sea with a few assured friends. The fleet fell into confusion, and separated; —some ships at once went home, the rest were assailed by the Spaniards, and returned discomfited, with the loss of one tall bark.

II.—THE VOYAGE OF THE GOLDEN HIND.

Impoverished by these disasters, it was not till the patent had nearly expired that Sir Humphrey procured the means to equip another expedition. With the assistance of Raleigh, now in high favour with the Queen, he collected a fleet of five ships. "We were in all," says the chronicler of the voyage, "two hundred and sixty men; among whom we had of every faculty good choice, as ship-wrights, masons, carpenters, sn ths, and such like, requisite to such an action; also mineral-men and refiners. Besides, for solace of our own people, and allurement of the savages, we were provided with music in good variety; not omitting the best toys for morris-dancers, hobby-horses, and many like conceits." Before Gilbert sailed, on the 11th June 1583, the Queen sent him a jewel, representing an "anchor guided by a lady," as a token of regard. In spite of the desertion of the bark which Raleigh had equipped, the fleet reached Newfoundland in safety by the end of July. The first glimpse of the coast—a bleak stretch of rocks looming through a dense fog—was disheartening; but a more favoured spot was soon after reached, where the weary mariners were charmed with the sight of fresh green foliage, bright flowers, and berry-bearing plants. It was just at the close of the fishing season, of which they observed a significant sign in "the incredible multitude of sea-fowl hovering over the bank, to prey upon the offal of fish thrown away by the fishermen." They were well received by the ships of various nations at St. John's. Sir Humphrey at once landed, took formal possession of the country in the name of the Queen, amid a salvo of ordnance from the vessels in the anchorage, and gave grants of land to various persons. Disaffection, unfortunately, broke out among his crew, one half of whom returned to England. With the rest he set out to explore the coast towards the south. He sailed in his little ten-ton cutter, the *Squirrel;* the larger ships, the *Delight* and the *Golden Hind,* following as near the shore as they dared. The summer was spent in examining all the creeks and bays, noting the soundings, taking the bearings of every possible harbour, and carefully surveying the rugged coast, at great risk of destruction. The admiral was satisfied with the appearance of the land. A lump of ore which was picked up was pronounced by the mineral-men to be silver, to the delight of the crew. One night towards the end of August there were signs of a gathering storm, though the weather was fair and pleasant. It was afterwards remembered that, " like to the swan, that singeth before her death, they in the *Delight* continued in the sounding of drums and trumpets and fifes, also the winding of cornets. and haughtboys, and in the end of their jollity left with the battell and ringing of doleful bells." Two days after, the tempest broke upon them. The *Delight,* the largest vessel in the fleet, struck upon a rock and went down in sight of the other vessels, which were unable to render any help. A large store of provisions and Sir Humphrey's papers were lost. The *Hind* and the *Squirrel,* which had made a narrow escape, were now alone. The weather continued boisterous, winter had fairly set in, and the cold became more cruel. Provisions running short, both crews were put on short allowance, and used to condole with each other by signs, pointing to their mouths and exhibiting their thin and tattered clothes. Not without much pressure from his men Sir Humphrey was persuaded to abandon his explorations for the present, and to return to England. He did his best to cheer the drooping spirits of his companions, going from one vessel to the other "making merry;" speaking hopefully of future expeditions to Newfoundland, and declaring that, on hearing what had been done, the Queen would provide the money for another voyage. Those in the *Golden Hind* besought him not to expose himself to shipwreck in a vessel so slight, frail, and overloaded as the *Squirrel;* but he refused to quit the men with whom he had already passed through so many storms and perils. Soon afterwards the weather became dark and lowering. The sailors, oppressed with a vague sense of coming ill, declared that they heard strange voices in the air, and beheld fearful shapes flitting around the ship. The seas were more "outrageous" than the oldest mariner had ever known before. "On Monday the 9th September," says Hayes, "in the afternoon, the frigate was near cast away, oppressed by the waves, but at that time recovered. Giving forth signs of joy, the general, sitting abaft with a book in his hand, cried out unto us in the *Hinde,* so often as we did approach within hearing, 'We are as near to heaven by sea as by land,' reiterating the same speech,—well becoming a soldier resolute in Jesus Christ, as I can testify he was. The same Monday night, about twelve of the clock, or not long after, the frigate being ahead of us in the *Golden Hinde*, suddenly her lights were out, whereof as it were in a moment we lost the sight; and withal our watch cried, 'The general is cast away!'—which was too true."

Thus perished Sir Humphrey Gilbert, to the end resolute in a "purpose honest and godly as was this, to discover, possess, and reduce into the service of God and Christian piety, those remote and heathen countries of America."

The *Golden Hind* survived the storm, and bore the tidings of the disastrous fate of the expedition to England. For a time all projects of colonization in that rugged and inhospitable island were abandoned. A number of vessels, however, still resorted to the fishings during the summer season; and, occasionally, one or two crews wintered on the island. In 1612, Alderman Guy, a rich merchant of Bristol, projected a settlement in Newfoundland. A company was formed, under a royal patent, and three vessels conveyed Guy and a small body of colonists to their new home. In spite of the exertions of the governor, and the supplies from the company in England, the colony languished. The settlers endeavoured to trade with the natives; but they were timid and suspicious, and "shrank from the white men." There were constant disputes between the planters and the fishermen. The residents charged the visitors with wasting the trees for fuel and fishing stages, and silting up the harbours with ballast. The fishermen retorted that the planters sought to monopolize the fisheries, which had been free from time immemorial. Pirates took advantage of these quarrels to despoil both parties, and to levy black-mail on all vessels approaching the coast. In ten years, the colony had lost at the hands of these marauders £40,800 in money, and more than a thousand men slain or enslaved.

In 1621 the colony received a fresh impulse from the patronage of Sir George Calvert, afterwards Lord Baltimore, a man holding high office in England, and enjoying the confidence of King James. A sincere Roman Catholic, he was anxious to provide a peaceful retreat from persecution for the adherents of that religion, and selected the southern promontory of Newfoundland as a suitable spot. He despatched Captain Edward Wynne with a well selected band, to lay the foundation of the new settlement. So sanguine were the colonists, that on the bleak rocky shores, wrapped in saline vapours and swept by withering blasts from the ice-fields, they already saw in fancy, not only fields of waving corn, but vineyards bursting with rich clusters of the grape. Nor had the old hallucination died out. The "prospect of mines" was excellent; and there was "a certain report of a Portugal that had found one pearl worth 300 ducats."

Lord Avalon, son of Lord Baltimore, arrived to rule the colony; and soon after the generous patron himself appeared upon the scene. He came just in time to chastise some French ships which had been annoying the settlers. Victory proved nearly as costly as defeat; for so many Frenchmen were made captive, that, provisions being somewhat scarce, Lord Baltimore was at a loss how to maintain them without stinting his own people. The presence of this nobleman exercised a happy influence. He was earnest in promoting habits of domestic order and economical industry, discountenanced the idle visions of El Dorado, and gave the planters every encouragement to apply themselves to the tillage of the soil and the creation of a steady commerce. Nor were his benefits limited to advice. He impaired his estate to the extent of £25,000, in advancing the interests of the colony. In spite of these advantages, it proved a failure. In 1629 Lord Baltimore wrote to the King that he had met with difficulties which he could no longer resist, and had resolved to seek some warmer and more promising spot on the shores of America. He described the winter in Newfoundland as intolerably severe, both land and sea being frozen for nearly eight months. His house had been an hospital nearly all the winter. Out of the hundred settlers, fifty were sick in bed,—he himself amongst the number. Nine or ten had died. Broken in health, disappointed in his hopes, impoverished in fortune, he was still bent on founding a settlement. "My inclination," he wrote, "entirely carries me to proceedings in plantations;" and he besought the King to give him a grant of land in Virginia, whither he desired to remove with forty persons. King James urged him to return to England, "seeing that men of his condition and breeding are fitter for other employments than the forming of new plantations, which commonly have rugged and laborious beginnings." The brave old nobleman was of another mind. He looked for no personal profit from the project; but he had set his hand to the work for the good of others, and he would not withdraw from it. So he departed, with his little company, from the windy shore of rocky Avalon, to found a happier and more enduring colony in Maryland.

Notwithstanding the failure of these systematic attempts at settlement, the number of colonists on the island gradually increased, so that in 1653 it was estimated that there were fifteen stations, including three hundred and fifty families. The cod-fisheries also throve, and have always formed the chief resource and main-stay of the colony. From the middle of February to June, the hardy and intrepid fishermen, in small barks of from fifty to a hundred tons, pursue the seal among the seas of Newfoundland and Labrador, braving the fierce winds, the arrowy sleet and blinding snow, the over-mastering currents, and dreadful onset of crashing icebergs. From June to November the cod-fishery occupies their energies. In the depth of winter the fishermen and their families desert their rude hovels of bark or turf upon the beach, and retire into the recesses of the forest, where they find shelter from the blasts, and fuel for their fires. Several well-to-do towns form the chief stations of the trade in fish and oil.

The Foundation of Virginia.

I.—ROANOKE.
II.—CAPTAIN JOHN SMITH.
III.—SUNSHINE AND SHADE.

The Foundation of Virginia.

I.—ROANOKE.

UNDISMAYED by the calamities which befell the expedition of Sir Humphrey Gilbert, and full of generous faith in his projects of colonization, Sir Walter Raleigh resolved upon another attempt to found an English settlement in America,—not on the gloomy shores of the icy gulf, but in some kindly region of the warm and balmy south. Receiving a liberal patent for a colony from the Queen, he intrusted its execution to two tried and worthy captains, Philip Amadis and Arthur Barlow, who, in 1584, led two vessels well laden with men and provisions to the New World. After two months' sail (for they steered their course by the Canaries and West India Islands), a fragrant odour, "as of a rich and delicate garden," warned them that, although still unseen, land was not far distant, and wooed them to approach. They were then off the coast of Florida, but had to sail northwards one hundred and twenty miles before they found a suitable harbour. The first aspect of the country was like a glimpse of

Paradise to the storm-tossed voyagers. It was the season in which the land put forth its most lavish charms. The shores were covered with noble groves of cedar, pine, and cypress, richly festooned with clambering vines, which, in their wanton luxuriance, sent forth a thousand tendrils across the golden sands. The beach was strewn with clusters of purple grapes, which the waves plucked and carried to the ships, as though it were an offering of welcome to the strangers. The report of a gun startled a legion of snow-white cranes into the air; and when the English landed they found the woods swarming with game of every species. But no creature of their own kind was visible till the third day, when a canoe filled with natives suddenly approached. Some trifling presents gained the confidence of this simple people, who are described as "most gentle, loving, and faithful; void of all guile and treason, and such as lived after the manner of the golden age." Further acquaintance proved that simplicity might be combined with cruelty and deceit; that whole tribes had perished in domestic feuds; and that their art of war was, to invite their enemies to a feast of peace and murder them in the hour of confidence. The natives, however, gave good entertainment to the English, who were much interested by the sight of the rare jewels and plates of yellow metal which they wore. After a summer spent in pleasant wanderings among the "hundred islands" of North Carolina, the fleet returned to England, to sing the praises of the promised land which fortune had bestowed on them, and which, in honour of the Queen, was called Virginia. The island of Roanoke was chosen as the head-quarters of the settlement.

In the following year a fleet of seven vessels, under the command of Sir Richard Grenville, conveyed a body of one hundred and eight emigrants to Virginia. The admiral spent but a short time abroad, returning to England with a rich cargo of furs and pearls, and a Spanish prize, which he captured on the way. Short as was his stay, his rashness led him to commit an act which, in the end, proved very fatal to his countrymen. A silver cup was stolen in one of the Indian villages, and because it was not quickly restored, Grenville burned the wigwams of the natives, and laid waste their crops. The injury was never forgiven.

Mr. Ralph Lane, who was left in command of the colony, confirmed the former glowing accounts of the country. "It is the goodliest soil," he wrote, "under the cope of heaven. If Virginia had but horses and kine, and were inhabited with English, no realm in Christendom were comparable to it." Hariot, an eminent mathematician, who accompanied the expedition, supplied more specific information as to the land, its people, and its resources. He noted the value of three new plants,—tobacco, maize, and the potato; and also the want of combination among the natives. The wonder and awe with which the

English were regarded on account of their fire-arms, and other strange instruments, Hariot sought to turn to account, by impressing on the natives the truths of his religion. Wherever he went he displayed the Bible and explained its meaning. The Indians, ever ready to hail a new divinity, accepted the sacred volume as the idol of the white man, and kissed and hugged it as a charm against evil. As the English were all men, and as during their stay none of them succumbed to disease or wounds, it was supposed that they were not born of woman, and that they were some ancient race risen from the slumber of ages. This surmise was quickly followed by the dark suspicion which always disturbs the mind of the savage when he first learns his helplessness before the civilized man: "Lo, these are come to kill our people and possess the land!" The Indians resolved not to yield without a struggle. To deceit, the arm of weakness, they resorted for protection. Menatonon, a crafty chief, saw that the new comers were mad about gold, and told them of a region beyond the setting sun where there were such inexhaustible mines of the precious metal that the natives adorned their houses with it. Lane was impatient to ascend the rapid current of the Roanoke and penetrate to this source of boundless wealth. Menatonon undertook to provide supplies of provisions along the route. But as the English advanced they found only empty wigwams and wasted fields. In three days their slender store of food was consumed. Blinded with the lust of gold, they could not see that the Indians were luring them to destruction. Lane had some glimmering of the truth, and urged them to return. "No," was their answer; "while we have yet two dogs to eat we will go on." A sudden shower of arrows from an ambuscade, however, drove them into retreat. On their way back to Roanoke they were glad to eat their dogs.

Deterred by Lane's reappearance from attacking the settlement, the Indians would have left their lands unplanted, in order to starve the English, had not one of their chiefs dissuaded them. The suspicions of the settlers were by this time alive. Lane, a headstrong and unscrupulous man, obtained an audience of Wingina, the supreme prince, and his chiefs, and slew them during the conference. Open war followed. The English, afraid to venture beyond their station, fell into despondency. They gave themselves up for lost, when they saw the bay whitened with the sails of a large fleet, which they imagined to be Spaniards. It proved to be Sir Francis Drake on his way home from a successful raid upon the Spanish settlements. He supplied his unhappy countrymen with a bark and several pinnaces, in order that they might have the means of quitting Roanoke when they chose; but a dreadful storm arose, and the vessels were all lost in "the wild road of their bad harbour." Supplies from

England were now long over-due, and in despair Lane and his companions eagerly accepted Drake's offer of a homeward passage in his fleet.

Within a few days a ship arrived laden with abundant provisions. Finding the little fort a desolate ruin, it at once departed, fearful that the destroyer might be still lurking on the shore. A fortnight afterwards came Sir Richard Grenville with three well-furnished ships. Unwilling that England should forfeit her right to the country, he landed a body of fifteen men on the island of Roanoke, and returned to England to report the mysterious disappearance of the colony.

It shows the brave, steadfast heart of the man, that even now Raleigh did not despair. A series of disasters had overthrown his schemes, but they were due to accident. It had been proved beyond question that the soil was of exuberant fertility, and that the climate was not unhealthy. It was just the spot, Raleigh argued, for an agricultural settlement. So he got together a company of emigrants, and despatched them with their wives and families, under Captain John White, to found the "city of Raleigh," on the rich shores of the Bay of Chesapeake. Unable, however, to fulfil that design, they resumed the plantation of Roanoke. The spectacle upon which their eyes fell when they landed on the island was ominous of evil. They beheld a group of ruined huts half buried in a rank growth of weeds, and tenanted by the wild deer and the cony. Here and there a ghastly human skull grinned on a crumbling threshold; or a human bone, bleached by exposure, gleamed through the lush-green herbage. A sense of vague, undefined danger, fell upon them, which even the stoutest heart could not shake off. They would fain have been at peace with the Indians; and, by direction of Sir Walter Raleigh, Manteo, a well-disposed chief, was baptized, and invested with the rank of a feudal baron, under the title of Lord of Roanoke. But an inexorable destiny seemed to precipitate them into feuds with the natives. In revenging the murder of one of their chief men, the settlers, in the darkness of night, put to the sword several members of a friendly tribe, whom they mistook for enemies. At the urgent desire of his companions, White consented to go to England for fresh reinforcements and supplies. He left on the island eighty-nine men, seventeen women, and several children, including his own grand-daughter, Virginia Dare, the first offspring of English parents born in America.

When White reached England, he found the nation engrossed with one subject. The existence of Protestantism, the independence of England was at stake, and no one could spare a thought to anything save the defence of the kingdom and the defiance of Pope and Spaniard. The Armada had to be destroyed; and even when that feat was accomplished, some time passed before funds could be procured for the little colony. Raleigh, unable to meet the repeated demands on him, formed a Company to carry out the project.

Nearly three years after his departure from Roanoke, White returned, to find the settlement was again a desert. He and his men made the woods ring with bugle calls, familiar English songs, and friendly watch-words; but drew forth no response save the cry of the startled birds and the sighing whisper of the leaves. A gathering storm drove the explorers to their ships. Five successive expeditions were fitted out by Raleigh, at his own cost, to search for the lost settlers. To this hour their fate is unknown. Doubtless they were murdered by the natives; but one would fain believe the tradition, that a party of them, wandering from the fort in search of food, fell in with a tribe of kindly natives, who adopted the worn wayfarers as brethren. It is said that, several generations afterwards, evidence of this amalgamation was to be found in the mien and lineaments of the natives of one corner of the island. Roanoke, says Bancroft, is now almost uninhabited,—commerce has selected more secure harbours for its pursuits; the intrepid pilot and the hardy "wrecker" are the only tenants of the spot, where the inquisitive stranger may yet discern the ruins of the fort erected by the old colonists.

II.—CAPTAIN JOHN SMITH.

For sixteen years the Indians remained in undisturbed possession of Virginia. But it was too lovely and bountiful a land to be abandoned by the English. The sense of danger excited by the disasters which befell former colonists faded in the lapse of years; the richness and beauty of the country were always fresh in the minds of men. In 1605 a new colony was projected by an influential Company, and in the following year a band of one hundred and five emigrants entered the waters of the broad, majestic Chesapeake; and, sailing up a noble river for about fifty miles, planted their camp on a peninsula, to which, in honour of their king, they gave the name of Jamestown.

At first all went well. The settlers were delighted with the aspect of the country. Labour was an agreeable novelty, after the irksome idleness of a long sea-voyage. All set heartily to work, some to build a fort, some to clear the soil, and others to prepare freight for the returning ships. The Indians, at first restrained from molesting them by the peaceful counsels of their king,—who said, "They hurt you not, they take but a little waste land,"—after a time became impatient. When the colony was weakened by the absence of an exploring party, they fell upon it, and slew seventeen men. From the first there had been jealousy among the settlers, and open dissensions now broke out. Edward Wingfield, a weak, bad-hearted man, who had been chosen governor, sought to get rid of Captain John Smith, whose watchfulness and resolution hindered his own selfish and dishonest schemes. He trumped up a charge of disloyalty against Smith; but the stratagem recoiled upon his own head. After an impartial trial, Smith was acquitted, and the governor condemned to pay a heavy fine. When the squadron which had conveyed the colony to Virginia returned to England, a season of misery and privation ensued. The settlers, relying on the stores of the ships, had lived extravagantly, without heed for the morrow. To their dismay, they now found that their provisions were nearly exhausted. The undisciplined fertility of the land, although fair to the eye, supplied but slender food. The dread of Indian ambuscades deterred them from hunting in the woods. The rank and rotten vegetation bred disease, which was fostered by scanty and unwholesome fare. Half a pint of barley and half a pint of wheat boiled with water formed a day's allowance for each man. "Our drink," said one of them, "was unwholesome water, our lodgings castles in the air; had we been as free from all sins as from gluttony and drunkenness, we might have been canonized as saints." So rapidly did health and strength fail them, that within ten days after the fleet sailed, there were hardly ten men able to stand on their legs. Before three months were over, fifty had perished. In the height of their distress, the Indians used them kindly, and gave them food. But they soon learned to despise men who did nothing but bewail their lot, and tired of helping those who seemed unable to do anything for themselves. An incident, which at first appeared a calamity, served to restore the character of the white men in the eyes of the natives, and to form a bond of friendship between the two races.

The hero of this episode was Captain John Smith, the story of whose romantic and adventurous career is stranger than any fiction. When at school, he sold his satchel and books in order to run away to sea, but was detained by his father's death. The opportunity of "setting out on brave adventures," for which he had longed in boyhood, arrived while he was still a youth. He served with distinction in several foreign wars, always fighting, like a true knight-errant, to redress tyranny and succour the oppressed. Among other brilliant exploits, he once threw the Turks into a panic by fastening several thousand cartridges to a long rope extended in a line, and firing them all at once, so as to imitate a discharge of musketry, and lead the enemy to believe that their flank was turned. Taken captive by the Turks, he was sold "like a beast in the marketplace," and transferred to the service of a lady of rank. His mistress, moved to pity by his youth and gallant bearing, sought to mitigate his servitude by various indulgences. This reached her brother's ears, who, enraged at such sympathy for an enemy of his country, despatched Smith to a fortress in the Crimea, where he shared the tasks and kennels of a band of half-savage serfs. Goaded almost to madness by brutal usage, he one day flung himself upon his master, stabbed him, and mounting a horse that was at hand, dashed off into the woods, "God directing him in the great way of Castroyan." He escaped into Russia, and was on his way home to his " own sweet country," when he was drawn to North Africa by the prospect of joining in a war against the Moors. He engaged with much ardour in a plan for colonization in that part of the world; and when it broke down through the dishonesty of some of the agents, he transferred his services and his enthusiasm to the planting of Virginia. A valiant and skilful soldier; a hardy navigator; a firm, upright, and sagacious leader, he proved the saviour of the English settlers, and must be regarded as the real founder of the colony.

On his first arrival, Smith undertook the exploration of the country with a few companions. In the winter of 1606 he made an expedition up the Chickahominy River. A dense tangled brake spanning the stream compelled him to quit his canoe, and he pushed forward on foot with two Englishmen and two natives. A body of hostile Indians slew the two Englishmen as they lay asleep. Undaunted in the presence of two hundred savages, Smith turned to bay. Binding one of the Indian guides firmly to his arm, he used him as a shield against the arrows of the foe, twenty of whom he brought to the ground with his musket. He would have escaped, had he not sunk into a treacherous swamp. Even then the Indians, awed by his courage, and frightened by the thunder and lightning which he called forth at will, stood aloof. It was only when Smith, finding himself gradually descending into the slough, and preferring capture by the Indians to immediate suffocation, called to them for help, and flung away his gun, that they ventured to approach. They released him from his dangerous position; and, in return, he amused them by exhibiting his pocket-compass, and explaining how the quivering needle was his guide through the pathless forest. He also tried to make them comprehend the roundness of the earth, the cause of day and night, and the process of the spheres. The Indians began to think that their prisoner was no man, but a deity from the clouds. They led him in triumph to the seat of their monarch, the great Powhatton. The squaws and children poured forth to see the pale-faced warrior. The men greeted him with chants of victory, and rejoiced in the wild measures of their war-dance. Smith was lodged in a large wigwam, and a strong band of "braves" mounted guard over him. He was so well fed that he began to suspect they were fattening him for the table. In conversing with him, the Indians made no secret of their intention to destroy the colony. To deter them, he described the formidable weapons with which his friends were armed. As the Indians were somewhat incredulous, it was agreed that messengers should be sent to test the truth of his reports. He gave them one of his tablets, on which he had written a few words, desiring the settlers to frighten the savages with guns and fire-works, but not to hurt them. A day or two afterwards the messengers came back with most appalling accounts of the power of the people, who could make a bit of paper speak, who could blow a great tree into splinters half a mile off, and who wielded the thunder and the lightning as familiarly as the Indians their tomahawks and blow-pipes. The heads of the priesthood were called together, to declare the nature of this strange race; and for three days they wrought their magic spells.

At last Smith was carried before the Indian monarch, who received him amid all the pomp and splendour of his savage court. The Englishman saw before him a tall, majestic figure, of a sad aspect, clothed in robes of rich fur, and seated on a throne. Two daughters, gaily dressed, and adorned with heavy necklaces of beads, which hung down to their middle, and in which they rested an arm as in a sling, sat one on each side of the king. The grim

CAPTAIN JOHN SMITH A PRISONER.

courtiers, with their wives, were ranged around. A loud shout greeted the entrance of the captive. One of the ladies of the court respectfully handed him a basin of water for his hands; another tendered a bunch of feathers as a substitute for a towel. After a grand feast the council passed judgment on the white man, whom they regarded with mingled fear and admiration. They reverenced his power, but they doubted whether it was for good or evil. Their fears prevailed, and he was doomed to die. Two large stones were placed upon the ground. Several Indians seized their victim and placed his head upon the block. A dozen stalwart arms brandished as many clubs, waiting the signal to strike. Suddenly a piercing shriek rang through the hall. Pochahontas, the favourite daughter of the king, then budding into the early maturity of Indian womanhood, rushed forward, stooped over the Englishman, and clasped her arms round his neck, vowing that if they would not spare him she would share his fate! The noble bearing of the unhappy stranger, so calm in the face of death, so strong in his isolation, had quickened her compassion. Perhaps, too, with the confiding piety of woman, she discerned in him a being of a beneficent and superior order, by slaying whom her countrymen might bring a curse upon themselves. Powhatton and his councillors could not resist the appeal of Pochahontas; and in giving the stranger his life they sought to propitiate his good-will. Two days afterwards he was despatched, under a trusty escort, to Jamestown. He entertained his attendants with great kindness, and sent them back laden with gifts for his preserver and her royal father.

The Englishmen and the Indians were now brought into close and friendly relations. Every few days Pochahontas, with a number of companions, visited the fort, and brought baskets of corn for the garrison. The settlers were enabled to study the manners and feelings of the natives. At that time three chief tribes dwelt in the land,—the Powhattons, the Manuahoacs, and the Monacares. The empire of Powhatton had the widest borders. Daring, subtle, and ambitious, this prince had raised himself from a petty chief to be a great monarch. Many tribes had yielded to the force of his arms, and had been amalgamated with his people. The Manuahoacs and Monacares, afraid of a similar fate, had formed a close alliance, and waged incessant war against the aggressor. The various tribes were much the same in appearance. In figure, they were tall and shapely, at once strong and supple. Their hair was jet black; and their complexion, originally of a bright copper colour, was deepened to a more dusky hue by the application of grease and the juice of certain plants. They went clothed in mantles and aprons of deer-skins, and dyed their breasts and faces with fantastic streaks of red and blue. Wooden clubs and swords, bows of hazel with arrows of reed, blow-pipes, and frail shields of bark and sticks woven together with grass, were their only weapons. A few wigwams in a circle of stakes represented a town, the largest containing only thirty dwellings. To build a house, they planted a circle of flexible saplings, drew the tops together, and bound them with cord. A thatch of bark completed the edifice. Destitute of the arts, they were full of native wit and cunning. Endurance was their chief virtue. No torture could extract from them a moan or a tear. Their religion taught them to adore the elements; but they also acknowledged a Supreme Being, whose huge footprints they viewed with awe on a rock by the side of the River James. They had a dim conception of a future state, in which bad men suffered in everlasting ice, while the good basked in the never-ending summer of the happy hunting-grounds.

From the first landing of the colonists it had become daily more and more apparent that Smith was the foremost man among them, and the true guide and guardian of the settlement. No sooner was his back turned on the fort than the inmates fell into mischief and disorder. Thrice he had been absent exploring the country, and on each occasion he returned just in time to quell a mutiny that threatened to ruin the colony. Now it was President Wingfield, who having, with some confederates, seized the pinnace, and smuggled into it a large share of the slender stores of the starving settlers, was on the point of departing for England. The next time it was the new president, Ratcliffe, who had conspired with some others to desert the colony. When Smith returned from his captivity among the Powhattons, he found the settlers reduced by famine and disease to forty men; and of these the strongest were again preparing to escape with the pinnace. They were already on board, with sails hoisted to the breeze, but put back when Smith turned the guns of the fort upon them.

Thus passed the first nine months of colonial existence. The chief cause of the discord and misery which had arisen was the character of the emigrants. Of the original band of one hundred and five, only twelve were labourers and four artisans. The rest were decayed gentlemen, broken-down gallants, bankrupt tradesmen, serving-men, and loose fellows fresh from the stocks and the jail. They had looked forward to a life of prodigal ease, and had neither strength nor will for the toil and privation which must attend the early stages of colonial life. In nine months nearly a third of them had perished; and of the handful which remained, not ten were able-bodied men. It was about this time that Captain Newport arrived, with one hundred and twenty recruits, and supplies of provisions. Unfortunately, the new comers were of the same worthless kind as those who had preceded them,—men "ten times more fit to spoil than to maintain a commonwealth." Among the new arrivals were several gold-refiners, who pronounced the glittering yellow sand in a stream near the settlement to be gold. As yet only a few houses had been built, and barely four acres of land had been cleared; but instantly every other work, no matter how essential, was abandoned, in order to search for the precious metal. There was now "no talk, no hope, no work, but dig gold, wash gold, refine gold, load gold." Smith in vain remonstrated against this folly; and when Newport sailed for England with a cargo of the deceitful earth, "never did anything more torment him than to see all necessary business neglected, to freight such a drunken ship with so much gilded dust."

From the peak of the peninsula the colonists looked out upon the wide expanse of Chesapeake Bay, swollen with the waters of many noble rivers, and a myriad of smaller streams, which might be seen winding, like veins of silver, among the green hills, and gemmed with a thousand

"Summer Isles of Eden, lying in dark purple spheres of sea."

Availing himself of a brief season of repose which followed the departure of Newport and his golden freight, Smith explored the "Mother of the Waters," as the natives call the Chesapeake. In an open boat of three tons, exposed to wind and weather, with but a handful of companions, whose unruly spirit made them rather a hindrance than a help, and liable to the assaults of treacherous enemies, he accomplished a voyage of nearly three thousand miles, traversing the great bay, visiting many of its islands, surveying its chief tributaries and inlets, and penetrating far beyond the shores into the interior of the land. At the head of the bay he found an encampment of the Susquehannas, a tribe of gigantic stature, arrayed in the skins of bears and wolves, with the heads and teeth of the animals attached, in order to add a grim ferocity to their appearance. These simple giants could not be restrained from worshipping the travellers, with their guns and swords, as direct messengers from Heaven. Smith also made the acquaintance of the Mohawks, " who dwelt upon a great water, and had many boats and many men, and made war upon all the world," and of whom the feeble Algonquin tribes lived in much dread.

As usual, during his absence the colony fell into disorder; and on his return he assumed the nominal authority of the President, which he had already virtually exercised. He endeavoured to recall the settlers to a sense of their true mission, and to impress upon them the necessity of temperance and industry. He would tolerate no idleness;—" he who would not work might not eat." Some he employed to make glass, others to prepare tar, pitch, and potash. Leading a number of the " gentlemen" into the woods, he taught them to wield the axe, and himself set an example in felling trees and fashioning planks for building. At first the novelty and excitement of the exercise reconciled them to the work, and they found amusement in the thundering crash of the great trees as they came to the ground. But the axe soon blistered the delicate hands of the fine gentlemen, and the labour grew irksome and monotonous. "Many times every third blow had a loud oath to drown the echo." Smith cured this habit by counting the number of oaths, and for each ordering a can of cold water to be poured down the sleeve of the offender. Six hours in the day were spent in work, the rest might be given to pastime. Under this wholesome and energetic discipline, order and industry began to prevail in the settlement.

The arrival of Newport with a second body of recruits, and fresh instructions from the Company in England, somewhat disturbed the course of labour and contentment. The seventy new emigrants were of the same unsuitable class as the others; and Smith had to write home, entreating the Company, when they despatched another band of recruits, "rather to send but thirty carpenters, husbandmen, gardeners, fishermen, blacksmiths, masons, and diggers up of trees' roots, well provided, than a thousand of such as we have." The orders which Newport conveyed imperatively required that the country should be explored for gold, and threatened that unless the colonists sent back a freight equal in value to the cost of the last voyage (£2000), "they should be left in Virginia as banished men." Accordingly a gold-hunting expedition was projected, and, in spite of Smith's remonstrances, set out for the interior. The result was as he had predicted. After a fruitless search, the explorers returned to Jamestown, "deluded and disappointed, half sick, and all complaining of being sadly distressed with toil, famine, and discontent." The consequence of this diversion from the regular work of the colony was, that not more than thirty or forty acres were brought under cultivation; and, to avoid starvation, the English had to solicit food from the natives, upon whose charity some of them were degraded enough to live.

The friendly relations which Smith had established between the settlers and the Indians were also endangered by the folly and imprudence of Newport and his associates. A vain, boastful person, he sought to obtain favour in the eyes of Powhatton, and to elevate himself above the president, by lavish presents; which, of course, quite upset the "standard of currency." Amid this profusion of gifts, the natives began to undervalue the commodities of the English; refused to give them sufficient supplies of grain in exchange; and at length grew so petulant, through Newport's indulgence, that they helped themselves to what they wanted without the trouble of asking. Smith saw clearly what would be the result of this conduct. He seized a number of Indians

NEWPORT CROWNS THE INDIAN KING.

Page 53.

who had stolen some of his goods, and by whipping and imprisonment gave them such a wholesome lesson, that the colony was free from such molestation for some time to come.

When on a visit to Powhatton, Newport got up the farce of a coronation. The old king was delighted with the scarlet mantle and other regal raiment which the sea-captain produced; but when he was asked to kneel in order to receive the crown, he absolutely refused. He had never bent the knee to any one, and he vowed he never would. Some of the attendants had to lean upon his shoulders, and press his head forward, while the diadem was placed on his brow. When the English fired a volley in his honour, he jumped up in a fright, thinking his town was besieged. When he calmed down, he graciously presented Newport with his old cloak and worn-out shoes.

Not only had familiarity with the weapons of the English diminished the dread which the Indians entertained of them, but, through the folly of some of the colonists, they had procured and learned to use a number of guns. The dependence of the white men on the natives for food also excited the contempt of the sons of the forest, who now cherished the idea of sweeping them from the country. But for Smith, the colony would doubtless have perished long before under the tomahawks of the aborigines. Upon this resolute and courageous man, whom no craft could overreach, no surprise could baffle, no danger could daunt, the Indians looked with awe and veneration as a superior being. He seemed to bear a charmed life. They recollected how desperately he had defended himself when taken captive in the swamp, and how they had been moved to spare his life as if by the instigation of the gods. It was told, too, how once, when assaulted by a hostile tribe, he seized the chief by his long lock of hair, and placing a pistol against his breast, led him forth in the sight of all his followers, who were so awed by the daring and suddenness of the act, that they threw down their arms, and propitiated the white brave with gifts. They had tried in vain to poison him. A huge, stalwart Indian, once flung himself suddenly upon Smith, and both fell into the water; but, after a fierce grapple, Smith rose to the surface, and his antagonist never re-appeared. An accident led them to believe that he was not only himself above the penalties of mortality, but that he had the power of restoring the dead to life. An Indian prisoner having been confined in a small hut where there was a charcoal fire, and no escape for the vapour, was, of course, thrown into a state of stupor; from which Smith revived him by carrying him into the fresh air, and administering brandy and vinegar. To the simple natives it appeared that the patient had been brought back from the happy hunting-grounds.

The Indians, therefore, looked upon Captain Smith as the one obstacle to their designs. Having tried in vain to bribe him to desert his countrymen, Powhatton resolved to surprise and capture him. The wily prince enticed him to his court by a flattering invitation, and besought him, with many assurances of affection, to put away his guns, for they alarmed his subjects so much, that "if but a twig broke, they cried out, 'Here comes Captain Smith!'" Smith suspected the treacherous plan, and determined to be beforehand with the king. He would have seized Powhatton, had the chief not taken the alarm and fled with his family. The English, lulled into false security by the departure of the Indians, began to load their boats with grain, and might have fallen under the clubs of the Powhattons, had not their guardian angel Pochahontas apprised them of their peril. The English thus fore-warned were forearmed, and the natives, seeing that they were on their guard, did not molest them.

The danger of assault by the Indians having thus been averted, the colony enjoyed a brief interval of prosperity and repose, which was brought to an end by two deadly foes. The one was a legion of rats, which secretly invaded their store-houses and consumed their food. The other was the "insufferable sloth and unreasonable perverseness" of a number of the colonists, who defied authority, and would not bear their share in the toils and burdens of the settlement. At this critical period an explosion of gunpowder inflicted a terrible wound on the president. Unable to procure surgical aid in Jamestown, and in peril of his life by poison or assassination at the hands of his enemies, Smith reluctantly returned to England. He left behind him more than four hundred and ninety persons, of whom at least one hundred were well trained soldiers; a sufficient store of arms and ammunition; numerous flocks and herds; and a harvest newly gathered.

Just before Smith's departure seven ships arrived from England, with four hundred emigrants, bringing word that the Company had been again re-organized;— that Sir Thomas Gates, Sir George Somers, and Captain Newport, had been appointed to administer the affairs of the colony until Lord Delaware, the new governor, arrived; but that, as far as was known, the three deputies had perished in a dreadful storm which had separated their vessel from the rest of the fleet. The former president being thus deposed, and the new magistrates to all appearance drowned, anarchy ensued. The dissensions of the colonists provoked the hostility of Powhatton, who had no longer the fear of Captain Smith before his eyes. There were neither houses nor food for the new settlers. Famine and disease played havoc with the colony, which was now reduced to a band of sixty wretched, haggard creatures, who, having eaten every living thing upon the settlement except each other, endeavoured to prolong existence on roots and berries, with now and then a few small fishes.

Such was the situation of the English in Jamestown when Somers, Gates, and Newport arrived. They had been wrecked on the shores of Bermuda, had sojourned in that lovely island for nine months, and had crossed to Virginia in a couple of vessels which they had built of cedar, and in which there was but a single iron bolt! Of the four hundred and ninety persons whom Smith had left on the island, the sixty who remained were little better than living skeletons, in whose breasts all hope had died out. They would listen to no other course than to desert the settlement, sail for Newfoundland, and there seek for food and the means of return to England. Four pinnaces received the miserable band, and fell down the stream with the current. The fugitives were waiting for the turn of the tide to continue their voyage, when their eyes were gladdened by the sight of the long-boat of Lord Delaware, who had arrived with three well-stored ships. They at once bore up the helm, and, favoured by the wind, were that night again in the fort, which, but for the interference of Sir Thomas Gates, they would have burned on leaving.

III.—SUNSHINE AND SHADE.

When Lord Delaware arrived, he knelt on the strand in prayer; and the restoration of the colony was inaugurated by a solemn thanksgiving. Then with cheerful alacrity all applied themselves to their respective tasks. Houses were repaired and new ones reared. Fences were made good, and fields reclaimed after long neglect. The hours of labour were from six in the morning to ten, and from two to four in the afternoon. At the beginning and close of every day the bell sounded for prayers, and all flocked to the little church, built on rough pine columns fresh from the forest, and adorned with festoons of wild-flowers. A common stock was established, and a fixed allowance of food was served out to each settler. A code of minute regulations was enforced, which ranged from grave offences against religion and society, to the profane swearing of soldiers and the gossip of scandal-mongers.

Hopeful, however, as now appeared the prospects of the colonists, it was but a passing gleam of sunshine which cheered their situation, and vanished in the gloom which quickly fell upon them. Lord Delaware's broken health compelled him to quit the country. The settlers, sobered for a time by the dangers from which they had been so providentially rescued, quickly relapsed into their former idle and wanton habits. Sir Thomas Dale, the new governor, an upright but stern ruler, established martial law. Under Captain Argal, a deputy-governor, who acquired supreme authority on the return of Dale to England in 1616, the condition of the colony became intolerable. There were no limits to the tyranny and extortions of Argal and his faction. The food distributed to the settlers was "loathsome, and not fit for beasts." They were glad to still the pangs of hunger by eating dogs and vermin. A famishing wretch stole a quantity of meat, and was chained to a tree till he died from want. Slight offences were punished by slavery for a number of years. Many sought relief among the savages from the cruelty and oppression of their own countrymen, while others hid themselves in the woods or in caves of the earth. Lest these things should be revealed in England, letters were suppressed, and men were detained in Jamestown by force.

Upon the accession of Sir George Yeardley to the office of president, in 1619, commenced a happier era. Under his mild and liberal sway the settlers devoted themselves with energy and success to the development of the resources of Virginia. Hitherto their labour had been misdirected, for it had been given to the production of commodities such as ashes, soap, glass, and tar, with which the European market was already adequately supplied. In tobacco they found a staple which was the peculiar possession of the colony. At first it was cultivated merely as a temporary measure to procure funds for the settlement, until the vines and silkworms, of which great hopes were entertained, began to be productive. The Company at home joined with the Council on the spot in denouncing that "scurvy and contemptible weed," which was distracting attention from more certain and enduring employments. King James, as might be expected from the author of the "Counterblast to Tobacco," was much troubled that the colony should be "wholly built upon smoke," and commanded his subjects in Virginia to give more care and time to the production of potash, salt, wine, and silk. But planters saw that tobacco was by far the most profitable article they could cultivate; and tobacco gradually engrossed the industry of the settlers. It not only covered the fields, but invaded the streets and squares of the town. In their haste to be rich, the English neglected to sow a sufficient quantity of grain, and would have been starved had they not obtained supplies from the Indians. Thenceforward tobacco became not only the staple, but the currency of Virginia; and the aroma of the weed clings to every page of its history. Six or seven years afterwards cotton was introduced, and proved a successful experiment.

Hitherto Virginia had been the resort of adventurers, who were willing to sacrifice a few years in a distant land in the hope of gaining the wealth with which they could spend the remainder of their days in ease and luxury in the old country. Few, if any, were more than birds of passage, or were willing to look upon Virginia as their home for life. But now the colony entered on a new stage of existence. It acquired permanence and stability by the adoption of a valuable staple of commerce, and the admission of the settlers to a voice in the administration of their affairs. Men went out for the purpose of establishing themselves permanently on the soil; and women followed. The Company induced "ninety agreeable persons, young and incorrupt," to emigrate. They found husbands as soon as they arrived, who were only too glad to repay to the Company the costs of their passage. Next year a second party of young women reached Virginia; and the Company were able to make a profit out of the transaction. Such was the demand for partners, that the settlers were willing to pay 150 pounds of tobacco as the expense of the voyage, instead of 120 (equal to about 150 dollars at the present day), which was the original tariff. "Thus domestic ties were formed: virtuous sentiments and habits of thrift ensued; the tide of emigration swelled,—within three years fifty patents for land were granted, and 3500 persons found their way to Virginia."

For many years the English lived not only on peaceable, but friendly terms with the Indians. The bond of amity between them, it was believed, had been rivetted securely when the Princess Pochahontas was married to John Rolfe, a young Englishman, who, moved by a voice which sounded daily and hourly in his ears, laboured "for the conversion of the unregenerate maiden;" and finding love a subtle agent in the pious work, took her to wife after she had been baptized. The young couple visited England, where, after exciting the admiration and affection of all who knew her, the young heroine died, on the eve of returning to her native land. Powhatton did not long survive his favourite child. His brother, Opecancanough, who succeeded to the throne, distrusted and hated the English, but dissembled his feelings. From their first landing, the English did not neglect to preach the gospel to the heathens. Hariot, Hunt, Rolfe, and Whitaker, were distinguished for the zeal and earnestness with which they devoted themselves to the conversion of the Indians; but their labours yielded little apparent fruit. Among those upon whom some impression seemed to have been made was Opecancanough; but this was only part of the crafty Indian's scheme of deception.

Confident in the good-will of the natives, and eager to pursue the cultivation of tobacco, the settlers gradually abandoned the precaution of living together within the walls of the fort, and dispersed over the surrounding country. The Indians, conscious of their weakness in open battle, resolved to take advantage of the scattered situation of the English, and to fall upon them by surprise. The design was planned with the utmost secrecy. The traitors made no change in their intercourse with the settlers. On the forenoon of the day of the massacre they visited the English in their huts, and traded and sat at meat with them. On a sudden the signal was given. In an instant each village was swarming with Indians, who came from every side. The settlers, unarmed and unsuspecting, hemmed in on every side by their treacherous foes, fell an easy prey to the Indian tomahawks. Not content with murder, the butchers mangled the corpses of the victims. Not even a woman or a child was spared. In one hour three hundred and forty-nine persons were cut off. Jamestown, however, was saved by a happy accident. A converted Indian gave warning to an Englishman, who had been kind to him, the night before the attack; and the chief station, containing the bulk of the settlers, was thus enabled to offer an armed resistance, which the Indians did not dare to face.

This was a great blow to the colony. The English deemed it prudent to abandon the cultivation of remote fields, and concentrated themselves once more around Jamestown. Eighty settlements were reduced to six. From the extreme of confidence the English passed to the other extreme of hatred and suspicion. No peace was possible with a people who had so ruthlessly betrayed them. "Without a doubt," wrote the Council in 1623, "either we must drive them, or they us, out of the country." Successive Acts of Assembly imposed on settlers the duty of assailing the Indians at stated periods of the year; and heavy penalties were visited on all who held any intercourse with them. Nor were the Indians backward in making reprisals, though their incursions were generally attended with great loss to themselves. For a score of years this state of things continued.

Opecancanough had now passed by nearly thirty years the term of life allotted to man. His tall frame was bowed, his eyes were dim; but the old fire burned within his breast, and he still cherished an inextinguishable hatred of the white man, before whose growing power the glory and empire of his race were visibly declining. He was on the eve of death, and he resolved before his dissolution to muster all the strength of his people in a last convulsive effort to annihilate the strangers. The onset was commenced, and five hundred victims had been slain in the outer settlements, when the Indians suddenly fled, dismayed at their own deed, and at the recollection of their weakness to cope with the English, who had now recovered from their surprise, and were advancing against them. A fierce war ensued. Opecancanough died a captive, and the Indians were decisively subdued. They humbly sued for peace, and withdrew to the recesses of the interior, beyond the reach of the English, who thenceforth were rarely disturbed in their settlements.

As the Indians disappeared, the negroes entered on the scene. In 1620 a gang of negroes was landed in Virginia by a Dutch man-of-war, and attached the disgrace and misery of an unhallowed institution to the soil. For many years the number of negroes was very limited, and did not influence the character of the colony, which had now surmounted the diseases of infancy, and had passed into the period of robust and growing youth. From 3000 settlers in 1628, the number rose to 20,000 in 1660. Twenty churches had been erected; and a free school was open, not only to the children of the settlers, but of the Indians. The rich soil, disciplined by careful culture, yielded lavish harvests of grain and fruit. Tobacco flourished, and became every year more valuable. The cotton crops were also good. Here is a glimpse of the homestead of "worthy" Captain Matthews (about 1658), who may be taken as a type of a thriving planter:—" He hath a fine house, and all things answerable to it. He sows yearly store of hemp and flax, and has it spun; he keeps weavers, and hath a tar-house; he causes leather to be dressed, and hath eight shoemakers employed in their trade. He hath forty negro servants, and brings them up to trades in his house. He yearly sows abundance of wheat, barley, &c.; kills store of beeves, and sells them to victual the ships when they come hither; hath abundance of kine, a brave dairy, swine in great numbers, and poultry."

The farms were situated at great distances from each other; and the wretched condition of the roads, which at the best were only bridle-paths or cattle tracks, rendered visiting a rare occurrence. Each proprietor, living in the midst of his retainers and slaves, exercised a sort of feudal authority, which was unrestrained by the criticism of neighbours, for neighbours he had none. An impetuous love of independence and impatience of control marked the character of the people. Wild sports were passionately followed; and the fertility of the soil and the geniality of the climate fostered a rude luxury.

Virginia was now fairly settled. Its people were "Virginians born," and not English colonists. Its planting had been accomplished. Of the future growth of the fair and noble seedling it is no purpose of this volume to speak.

The Colonization of New England.

I.—THE PILGRIM FATHERS.
II.—NEW PLYMOUTH.
III.—MASSACHUSETTS.
IV.—THE ENGLISH AND THE INDIANS.

The Colonization of New England.

I.—THE PILGRIM FATHERS.

THE colonization of New England was accomplished by men of a very different stamp from those who first settled in Virginia. The Pilgrim Fathers brought to the task tempers chastened by long suffering, bodies inured to toil and privation, and hands skilled in various handicrafts. Driven by the persecutions of Archbishop Bancroft to quit their native land and to seek refuge in Leyden, they began, after a residence of eleven or twelve years in that city, to contemplate another and more hazardous pilgrimage. With all their toil, they gained but a poor livelihood, and endured many hardships. This deterred many of their brethren in England from joining them, and led their children to disperse, in search of more kindly fortunes, over the Continent. The language of the Dutch had never grown familiar to their tongues, nor had they lost their abhorrence of the lax native fashion of spending the Sabbath. They could not bear to think that their sons and daughters would gradually be incorporated with the Dutch, and would in another generation or two forsake entirely their English speech and habits. And not least in their scheme of emigration, they were moved by a "great hope and inward zeal they had of laying some good foundation, or at least to make some way thereunto, for the propagating and advancing the gospel of the kingdom of Christ in these remote parts of the world; yea, though they should be but as stepping-stones unto others for performing of so great a work." Upon this plan they "pondered, debated, fasted, prayed, and finally came to the resolution to remove."

The industry and sobriety of the English congregation commanded the respect of the Dutch. "Never," said the magistrates of Leyden,—"never did we have any suit or accusation against any of them." When their intention of emigrating was first rumoured, the Dutch would fain have had them "go under them, and made them large offers;" but they were bent on joining or founding an English colony. At first they contemplated a settlement in Guiana; but finally they decided upon establishing themselves on the northern shores of Virginia. They procured a patent from the Virginia Company, but the King would give no further countenance to their scheme than a promise not to molest them as long as they behaved themselves. The terms which the Company exacted were very hard for the poor emigrants, each of whom would, at the end of seven years, receive for his entire services only a tenth of the dividend which the London merchants would gain on every £100 which they invested.

Two small barks—the *Speedwell* and *Mayflower*—were hired by the English in Leyden; but as they could carry only a portion of the band, the younger and more hardy were chosen to go out as pioneers. The rest were to remain, until the ships returned, under the charge of John Robinson, the pastor of the exiled congregation,—a man of a devout and lofty spirit, by nature gentle and kindly, yet not devoid of that firmness without which the most admirable qualities are of small account. Among the most notable of the emigrants were William Brewster, the venerable ruling elder; John Carver, who had contributed a large proportion of the expenses of the undertaking; William Bradford, still young in years but old in wisdom and experience; Edward Winslow, a thoughtful, amiable man; and Miles Standish, the best "linguist" as well as the best soldier in the party, who was the devoted friend of the congregation, although not a member of it. All the exiles were "well weaned from the delicate milk of the mother country, inured to the difficulties of a strange land, industrious and frugal." "It is not with us," said one of them, "as with men whom small things can discourage." A solemn fast inaugurated the enterprise. The emigrants were accompanied by the whole congregation to the place of embarkation.

They cheered each other with prayers and with the singing of psalms,—" which, indeed," says one of them, " was the sweetest melody that ever mine ears heard." Making for Southampton, the *Speedwell* joined the *Mayflower,* her consort, with a number of emigrants from England; and soon after, both sailed for America. Twice they had to put back, because the *Speedwell* required repairs; and the second time, seeing that the captain was afraid of the voyage, they dismissed her, and allowed those who wished to return to London. On the 6th September 1620, one hundred emigrants in the *Mayflower* sailed for the other side of the Atlantic.

Two months later, after a stormy and perilous voyage, the *Mayflower,* with tattered canvas and leaking sides, utterly incapable of weathering another gale, came in sight of the white sand-hills of Cape Cod, and, narrowly escaping destruction among the treacherous shoals and breakers, crept to an anchorage in a little bay. The emigrants had intended to arrive in the middle of September, but the unexpected accidents which had occurred had delayed them till the winter was just setting in. The country wore a " bleak and weather-beaten face." The inhospitable range of ice-clad rocks, the shifting sand-hills, the bare and stunted trees and rusty-looking brushwood, combined to give an air of desolation to the scene.

."The sea around was black with storms,
White were the shores with snow."

Having signed a solemn voluntary compact to devise and obey such laws as might seem best for the good of the colony, they elected John Carver governor for the year. An exploration on foot, conducted by sixteen men under Miles Standish, and occupying three days, disclosed no available site for a settlement. Another expedition of equal duration was made in the shallop, with similar want of success. They found traces of the natives, but saw none of them. They were fortunate enough to discover a quantity of maize stored up under ground. They also came upon a burial-place of the Indians, and, opening some of the tombs, beheld bones, weapons, and other relics of the dead. Continuing their search, they " found no more corn, nor anything else but graves." William Bradford, one of the explorers, venturing incautiously too near a tree, one of the boughs of which was bent down in a peculiar manner, with a noose fastened to the end of it, entangled his foot in the rope, and was suddenly jerked up in the air by one leg, to the amazement of his companions. This was a device of the Indians for snaring deer. The weather was bitterly cold, and the men were " tired with marching up and down the steep hills and deep valleys, which lay half a foot thick with snow." Many received the seeds of death in the hardships of this adventure.

The English now debated whether they should not remain where they were, at least for the present;

but the bleakness of the region, and the want of water, led them to renew their search for a more favourable spot. Governor Carver, Bradford, Winslow, Standish, and some others, with eight or ten seamen, again set out in the shallop. The cold was extreme; the water froze upon their clothes, and incased them, as it were, "in coats of iron." More graves, and a group of empty wigwams, indicated the neighbourhood of the natives. During the night strange noises were heard, which they attributed to wolves. Next morning a shower of arrows and a hideous yell were their first introduction to the savages. Standish, ready for any emergency, instantly discharged his musket at the leafy screen whence the missiles came. The others stood to their arms, and the assailants fled. Resuming their voyage, the explorers, for forty or fifty miles, sailed through a blinding storm of snow and sleet without finding a harbour. The gale rose, the sea swelled; their rudder was disabled, and they had to steer with oars. Crowding all sail, in order to reach a haven which the pilot professed to know, the mast snapped, and, with the canvas, was carried away. Night fell, and they drifted helplessly in the dark with a flood-tide. Destruction seemed inevitable, when, with much difficulty, they brought up the boat under the lee of a small rise of land. Miserable with wet and cold, a number of the men went on shore, heedless of the danger of meeting the savages. The dawn showed them that they were on a "small island, secure from Indians." The day was spent partly in repose and partly in repairing the disasters of the storm. The next day was Sunday; which, in spite of every consideration demanding haste, they kept scrupulously sacred, giving thanks to God for their deliverance, and rousing the echoes with their hymns of praise. On Monday (11th December, old style) they sounded the harbour, and found it well suited for shipping. They "marched also into the land, and found divers corn-fields and little running brooks,—a place very good for situation; and so returned to the ship again with good news to the rest of their people, which did much comfort their hearts." The choice of this site is still celebrated by the descendants of the Pilgrims on Forefathers' Day (which, however, by a miscalculation as to the new style, is held a day later than it ought to be); and the stone on which the explorers first set foot is regarded with pious veneration.

II.— NEW PLYMOUTH.

By the end of the week the *Mayflower* brought her company to spend the Sabbath in their future home. With nothing but a rude screen of leafless boughs between them and the blast, they hallowed the day with pious ordinances and abstinence from worldly labour. Next day (Monday, the 25th), it is recorded—not without exultation—that they went on shore, "some to fell timber, some to saw, some to rive, and some to carry; so no man rested all that day." The settlers were divided into families, and a plot of ground was assigned to each, as the site of a house and garden. The building of log-huts was carried on with great energy; but frost and storms often put a stop to work for days together, or undid what had been done. The Pilgrims now began to be in a sad plight. Enfeebled by the long sea-voyage in a narrow, crowded ship; worn by incessant toil and painful anxiety; exposed to the rigours of an almost polar winter; supplied with scanty and unwholesome food; ill-clad, ill-sheltered, poorly armed, and surrounded by savages whose hostility they dreaded, there was enough in their situation to create dismay, if not despair. But in the midst of all their sorrows and dangers, the stout-hearted, God-fearing exiles were full of faith and hope. "They knew that they were Pilgrims, and looked not much on these things, but lifted their eyes to heaven, their dearest country, and quieted their spirits."

A fatal sickness wasted the heroic band. The common-house was crowded with invalids. "It pleased God," says Bradford, "to visit us with a death daily. So very general was the disease, that the living were scarce able to bury the dead; and the well were not in any measure sufficient to tend the sick." In four months half the company was carried off. Carver was amongst the victims, and Bradford was chosen governor in his stead. The dead were buried in secret, and the graves were levelled and sown, in order that the Indians might not, by counting them, learn how sadly the colony was reduced in strength.

Early in March, to the solace of the Pilgrims, came "warm and fair weather, and the birds sang in the woods most pleasantly." They were relieved from the apprehensions of attack by the natives by the sudden appearance in their midst of Samoset, an Indian who had learned a little English of the fishermen at Penobscot, and who greeted them with the words, " Welcome, Englishmen!" From this friendly visitor the settlers learned that the district in which they had settled had been depopulated some years before by a fearful plague; that their nearest neighbours were the subjects of the sachem Massasoit, of whom he was one; and that towards the south-east dwelt the tribe of Nausets, who bore ill-will towards the English, because a party of that nation had kidnapped some of their people. Through Samoset and another Indian, named Squanto (who was one of those who had been kidnapped, but had afterwards escaped), negotiations were opened with Massasoit, which led to a visit from that chief. He was received by the settlers with due respect, and propitiated by a present of some trinkets, together with "a pot of strong water, a good quantity of biscuit, and some butter." A treaty of mutual friendship and protection was formed between Massasoit and the English, which remained in force for fifty-four years.

In the beginning of April the *Mayflower* returned to England; and we may be sure it was with heavy hearts that the colonists watched the lessening speck upon the ocean, which, when it disappeared below the horizon, broke, as it were, the last outward link which connected them with the old country. They were now left entirely to their own resources. From the store-pits of the Indians they had procured ten bushels of Indian corn, with which they sowed twenty acres, under the guidance of Squanto, who showed how to manure it with fish, after the native fashion. The summer brought abundance of grapes and berries. Wild-flowers of brilliant hue and fragrant odour added a charm to the scene. The fine weather was spent in exploring the country. A deputation went to pay their respects to Massasoit at his head-quarters; but, although cordially received, they were somewhat disturbed by the poverty and filth in which the great sachem lived. Three small fishes were served as a banquet for the two envoys and forty natives. Expeditions also visited Nauset, Namosket, and Boston Bay.

"All the summer there was no want." The rivers and bay supplied plenty cod and bass, and there was also "great store of wild turkeys and venison." The harvest turned out well, especially in the maize fields. Thirty new comers, who arrived from England in November, were gladly welcomed; for the diminished number of the little band required recruiting. The addition enabled them to show a bold front to the Indians; and when Canonicus, chief of the Narragansetts, sent a bundle of arrows wrapped in the skin of a snake, as a declaration of war, he was glad to retract the challenge when Governor Bradford returned the snake-skin filled with powder and ball. The second winter was spent in comparative comfort; but throughout the whole of the next two years the Pilgrims suffered from want of food. Their crops were poor; and their scanty stores were diminished by the inroads of a disreputable rabble of Englishmen sent out by Mr. Weston, one of the chief members of the Company at home, to form a rival colony. Men were often seen staggering from want of food; and but for the shell-fish on the beach, they would all have been starved. Sometimes they were for two or three months together destitute of bread or any kind of corn. At one time when they were reduced to one pint of corn,—which, being parched and distributed, gave to each person only five kernels,—several new colonists joined the settlement without bringing any contribution to their stores. The best fare the colony could then offer was "a lobster or a piece of fish, without bread or anything but a cup of fair spring water."

An arrival, of between sixty and seventy recruits, in the third year, threatened to aggravate the distress which prevailed; but, fortunately, the harvest proved plentiful, and "all had, one way or other, pretty well to bring the year about." It was during this year that the system of community of goods, under which, rather from poverty than choice, the settlement had started, was abandoned. The new plan, of giving every one a piece of land for his own benefit, "had very good success; for it made all hands very industrious, and so, much more corn was planted than otherwise would have been, and it gave far better content."

The Pilgrims this year experienced a "remarkable providence." A long and severe drought had parched the land and wasted the crops. The middle of summer arrived without any sign of relaxation, and they began to lose heart. In their distress they humbled themselves before God, in fasting and prayer. Their devotions lasted seven or eight hours. When they began the sky was bright and glaring; before they had finished clouds lowered overhead, and at the close of the service they walked home thankfully through a shower of rain. For fourteen days there fell "such soft, sweet, and moderate showers, as it was hard to say whether their withered corn or drooping affections were most quickened and revived."

The infant settlement had now got over some of its gravest difficulties. It was learning to adapt itself to the circumstances of its position, to guard against many of the hardships and privations which beset it, and to alleviate those which it could not avert. A visitor to Plymouth about this time would have seen a cluster of rude wooden cabins studding the gently sloping crown of a high bluff. Built of logs, with well-cemented seams, these dwellings afforded at least a snug shelter from the weather; and in their new prosperity the settlers had indulged themselves in the luxury of windows, which they formed by piercing holes in the walls and filling them with oiled paper. The houses, about thirty-two in number, were ranged chiefly in two rows, forming a tolerably regular thoroughfare, which, in memory of the first exile of the Pilgrims, was called Leyden Street. At the lower end stood a large wooden shanty, containing the common stores of the plantation. At the upper end rose a little hill, surmounted by a fort,—a square building, with a flat roof, which served as a platform for half a dozen cannon to command the surrounding country. From this eminence the visitor might survey the entire colony. The boats of the settlers might be seen at high tide dancing over the waters of the wide natural harbour, or at the ebb lying stranded among the rank sea-grass and black kelp of the muddy shoals. Beyond, the open bay, green and foam-flecked, stretched to the horizon. Nearer might be seen the little village of the Pilgrims nestling to the bosom of the hill, intersected by a rapid, brawling stream, and enclosed within a ring of stout palisades. Groups of settlers might be observed at work;—some in the irregular unfenced fields which had been rescued from the surrounding wilderness, digging, hoeing, or perhaps manuring the ground with loads of herring as bright as silver; others gathering crabs and oysters in the slime of the shallows, fishing for cod with net or line in the deep water, or ranging the dark pine woods in search of game. To work of some sort or another must every one put his hand. Plymouth was no place for idlers. On the Sabbath the settlers might be seen winding in procession up the village street towards the fort, the lower part of which served as a church. "They assemble," says De Rosiere, a visitor from the neighbouring Dutch colony of Long Island, "by beat of drum, each with his musket or firelock, in front of the captain's door; they have their cloaks on, and place themselves in order, three abreast, and are led by a sergeant without beat of drum. Behind comes the governor, in a long robe; beside him, on the right hand, comes the preacher, with his cloak on; and on the left hand, the captain, with his side-arms and cloak on, and with a small cane in his hand; and so they march in good order; and each sets his arms down near him. Thus they are constantly on their guard night and day."

By 1628 Plymouth was in a thriving condition. There were about one hundred and eighty inhabitants,

SABBATH-DAY IN NEW PLYMOUTH

"some cattle and goats, and many swine and poultry." Several children had been born in the settlement, which the English regarded as their permanent abiding-place. "It pleased the Lord to give the plantation peace and health and contented minds, and so to bless their labours as they had corn sufficient and some to spare to others, with what they first brought with them." Instead of being dependent on the Indians for supplies, they could now, out of their abundance, sell grain to the natives, receiving furs and other commodities in exchange. From a trading excursion up the Kennebec River, made in an open boat, Winslow and some others returned with "seven hundred pounds of beaver, besides some other furs, having little or nothing else but corn" to trade with. The settlers were thus enabled to despatch cargoes to England: and fifty English ships frequented the coast in the fishing season, thus enlarging their market for buying and selling. In their growing prosperity the settlers found the means of ridding themselves of the incubus of the proprietary in England, and purchased the freehold of their plantation. The gratification which they derived from their brightening prospects was, however, clouded by the news of the death of Robinson, their old and beloved pastor in Leyden.

III.—MASSACHUSETTS.

The success of the Plymouth colony, and the continued oppression of the Nonconformists in England, aided the colonization of New England. A Company was formed, under royal charter, to establish a colony at Massachusetts Bay. In 1628 John Endicott of Dorchester led nearly a hundred emigrants thither, who settled in Charlestown. In the following year two hundred more arrived. They found only a few mud hovels and log cabins, and one or two unproductive fields. The prevailing forest mocked their hunger with rank, unprofitable vegetation. The sun was scorching; the soil was parched; the wells were dried up. The wretched strangers sank day by day and died for want of a cup of cold water and a proper meal. Winter aggravated their sufferings; and above eighty, nearly half of the little colony, died before the spring. Meanwhile the tide of immigration flowed in rapidly. From fourteen to seventeen ships sailed from England to Massachusetts in 1630, and carried over nearly fifteen hundred persons, "many of them men of high endowments, large fortune, and the best education." They received a dismal greeting from the starving colonists. The provisions which the new comers brought with them were soon consumed, and then the distress became terribly fatal. Before December two hundred had perished, and one hundred had fled from the settlement in despair to England. Shell-fish served for meat; ground nuts and acorns for bread. It is said that just as Governor Winthrop was distributing to a poor man the last handful of meal, a ship bearing supplies hove in sight. The distress of the colony was now at an end, and a period of prosperity ensued. From Massachusetts sprang several other settlements, of which the chief were those of Rhode Island and Connecticut.

Although the people of Massachusetts had crossed the Atlantic to gain tolerance for themselves, they had no idea of practising it towards others. Consequently, when Roger Williams, "a young minister, godly and zealous, having precious gifts," proclaimed the sanctity of the conscience and the duty of religious toleration, the magistrates and ministers were instantly in arms against him. The favour which the youthful preacher gained in the eyes of the people of Salem only aggravated the dislike with which the authorities regarded him; and after a time a sentence of exile was passed upon him. It was the depth of winter when the tidings reached him, and he turned his steps from Salem in the midst of a blinding snow-storm. "For fourteen weeks he was sorely tossed in a bitter season, not knowing what bread or bed did mean." In his distress the Indians succoured him. He had always been their friend, and had learned their language in order to preach to them. They now received him as an honoured guest, and ministered to his wants. In this seclusion he formed his plans for the establishment of a colony where there should be an entire freedom from religious persecution. He chose Rhode Island, on Narragansett Bay, which he held as a gift from the Indian chief, a large domain, as the site of the colony; and proceeded thither with five companions in a frail canoe. He bestowed upon the place the name of Providence, desiring that it "might be a shelter for persons distressed for conscience." To his fellow-colonists he set a noble example of industry. "My time," he says, "was not spent altogether in spiritual labours, but day and night, at home and abroad, on the land and water, at the hoe, at the oar, for bread."

Reports of the rich fertility of the valley of the Connecticut had long been current in Massachusetts. In 1635 a body of settlers set forth to possess it. They numbered sixty, including women and children, and their path lay through the primeval forest. It was autumn before they started, and the journey proved unexpectedly long. The winter set in suddenly, and with extreme severity. The vessels which were to bring them supplies were frozen in the rivers. The ground was covered under a great depth of snow. The travellers suffered from want of shelter and food, and many of the cattle perished from the same cause.

Next summer, however, another expedition started for the same goal. The second band numbered about a hundred. The distance they had to travel was a hundred miles, and they moved at the rate of scarcely ten miles a day. Their march through the pathless woods was directed by a compass. They drove before them a herd of one hundred and sixty cattle, which supplied them with milk. They hewed their way through the tangled woods, and bridged with felled trees the streams which they could not ford. Each evening they pitched their tents by the side of a pleasant stream. The vigorous exhortations of their preacher, Thomas Hooker, and their own songs, beguiled the way. The fruitfulness of the region in which they settled repaid them for the toil of the journey.

Such were the early incidents of colonization in New England. After their first trials, however, the progress of the settlements was steady and continuous.

The soil of New England is not generally fertile. The winter engrosses half the year, and during its more austere periods covers the ground for months with an unmelted mass of snow. Such a land only stimulated the steadfast, patient industry of the colonists,—which, moreover, it did not fail to reward. The rough unyielding hill-side and niggard plains succumbed to the unremitting labours of the persevering settlers; but not until they had been taught the precious lessons of patience, frugality, and faith. "New England was rich in the want of gold." There was nothing to divert her people from the steady cultivation of her natural resources. The result was, that agriculture and commerce advanced surely, if not rapidly. A number of families from Yorkshire introduced woollen and cotton manufactures. The fisheries and timber trade yielded large profits, and in time ship-building was added to the occupations of the colony. The necessary hours of toil and habits of economy allowed little scope for luxury or sports. Devout and sober-minded, the people of New England were rigidly severe in enforcing the observance of religious rites, and in denouncing the vanities of the world. No one might "give offence to his neighbour by the excessive length of his hair, embroidered and needle-work caps, gold and silver girdles, immoderate great sleeves and slashed apparel." Dancing, gambling, and tobacco-smoking were utterly prohibited; and the man who uttered an oath had his tongue locked in a cleft stick for half-an-hour. Music, and the fine arts generally, were looked upon with disfavour; but the benefits of a liberal education were fully appreciated, and literature was cherished. "When New England was poor, and they were but few in number, there was a spirit to encourage learning." Harvard College was founded in 1636; and the first printing-press in the United States was established at Cambridge in 1639.

COLONISTS ON THE MARCH.

Page 87.

IV.—THE ENGLISH AND THE INDIANS.

Scrupulous as the settlers of New England had been in their dealings with the aborigines, they could not escape that apparently inevitable destiny which leads the white man and the coloured races to fatal misunderstandings. During the early years of the colony the English and the Indians remained on amicable terms. Towards the year 1638, however, the Pequods on the Connecticut began to waylay and murder straggling settlers, and open war at length broke out. About eighty Englishmen marched to assail the two chief camps of the enemy. Bancroft has graphically painted the terrible encounter:—" As the English boats sailed by the places where the rude works of the natives frowned defiance, it was rumoured through the tribe that its enemies had vanished through fear. Exultation followed, and hundreds of the Pequods spent much of the last night of their lives in revelry, at a time when the sentinels of the English were within hearing of their songs. Two hours before day the soldiers of Connecticut put themselves in motion towards the enemy, and as the light of morning dawned they made their attack on the principal fort, which stood in a strong position on the summit of a hill. A watch-dog bayed an alarm at their approach; the Indians awoke, rallied and resisted as well as bows and arrows could resist weapons of steel. The superiority of numbers was with them; and fighting closely, hand to hand, though the massacre spread from wigwam to wigwam, victory was tardy. 'We must burn them!' shouted Mason, and cast a firebrand to the windward among the light mats of the Indian cabins. Hardly could the English withdraw to encompass the place before the whole encampment was in a blaze. The carnage was complete: about six hundred Indians (men, women, and children) perished in an hour. Two only of the English fell in the battle. .... The remnants of the Pequods were pursued into their hiding-places: every wigwam was burned, every settlement was broken up, every corn-field laid waste. The few that survived (about two hundred), surrendering in despair, were enslaved by the English, or incorporated among the Mohegans and Narragansetts. There remained not a sannup nor squaw, not a warrior nor child of the Pequod race. A nation had disappeared from the family of man."

After this awful catastrophe the land had rest from savage violence for forty years. During that period the English did not neglect to exert themselves to educate and convert the Indians. The settlers subscribed to send missionaries amongst them. Schools were founded, and books in their own dialects printed for their use. The two Matthews, father and son, and John Eliot, distinguished themselves as zealous apostles to the natives. The latter established a community of Indians at Nantick, not far from Boston, where they were taught various industries, such as agriculture, flax and hemp dressing, and were instructed in the truths of Christianity.

Notwithstanding these manifestations of good-will on the part of the English, the Indians were oppressed with a sense of their own helplessness and distrust of the new comers. The soil which had belonged to them for generations had passed into the hands of the white men. Their fathers' bones lay in the lands of the stranger. True, every inch of ground had been bought and paid for; but to the Indians' mind, unable to appreciate the comforts of civilized life, appeared only the broad patent fact, that they were gradually being dispossessed of their birth-right,—that their hunting-grounds were being converted into fields and home-steads, and that there would soon not be an inch of ground which they could call their own. Over the camp fire the young Indians murmured indignantly at this prospect. Rumours of this gathering rage reached the English. A vague terror threw both parties into a sort of frenzy. The English believed that a general conspiracy to destroy them had been concocted by the Indians. The Indians attributed a similar design to the English. Each felt that a decisive struggle was at hand. A few petty hostilities and reprisals hurried them into a war to the death. Philip of Pokanoket, son of Massasoit, the chief who received the Pilgrims so affectionately, assumed the leadership of the Indians. The war was a perpetual series of ambuscades and skirmishes. The Indians were ever on the alert to cut off the stragglers on the roads, to fire on unguarded farm-houses, to surprise the reapers reposing in the fields, or the congregations engaged in worship. "Bloody Brook," near Deerfield, takes its name from a massacre of the English. The little stream then ran by the side of a few corn-fields which had been rescued from the surrounding forest. Here a picked body of young men, who were conveying the harvests of Deerfield to the lower towns, halted for a moment in order to give water to their teams, and to pluck the grapes which hung in rich clusters over the road. Suddenly there was a rustle among the tangled wild grass. Was it the wolf or the rattlesnake? In an instant a thousand Indian warriors started from the covert and let fly a cloud of arrows on the devoted little band of English. Each party fought from behind trees. The settlers, overpowered by numbers, were quickly mowed down. The foremost of them, turning round to encourage his comrades, saw, in despair, that only seven remained alive. To continue the contest was hopeless. Dashing their arms in the faces of the Indians they tried to escape. All, however, were shot down save one, who hid himself in the water, clinging to the trunk of an old tree which was lying on the edge of the stream, with his mouth just above water, and his head screened by the brush-wood. When night fell, and the Indians withdrew, he hastened to Hodley to report the massacre, of which he was the sole survivor.

While the natives carried on the war in this fashion, the English mustered their young men to go forth against the camp of the enemy and destroy them. No quarter was given on either side. Against the combined movements and continuous assaults of the English the Indians could not long make head. Without shelter and food they took refuge in the swamp, where the white men dared not follow them. "They prowled the forests, and pawed up the snow, to gather nuts and acorns; they dug the earth for ground-nuts; they ate horse-flesh as a luxury; they sank down from feebleness and want of food."

But King Philip was still undaunted. There was a mysterious ubiquity about his movements which terrified many of the English. Whenever there was an attack more daring, a carnage more appalling than ordinary, Philip was supposed to be there. His path seemed to be watered with blood and lit by blazing home-steads. At length his wife and child fell into the hands of the English. "My heart breaks," he cried in his agony, "and now I am ready to die!" Even his own men began to plot against him; and soon after he was shot by a treacherous Indian. His wife and child were sold into slavery.

Thus the Narragansetts shared the fate of the Pequods. Scarcely a hundred of them survived. The English had also suffered severely. Twelve towns were destroyed. Six hundred men were slain, and six hundred dwellings were laid in ashes. But after these calamities there was peace in the land.

Tragedies, somewhat similar in character, but less fearfully profuse in bloodshed, were enacted in most of the other settlements before the white men and the red men settled down into relations which were marked by mutual friendship, or at least indifference. This, however, is a page in the history of colonization which one reads with horror, and from which one turns with relief.*

* The truth of the assertion, that a gradual extinction has been the fate of the coloured aborigines, has been challenged by eminent authorities; and it is satisfactory to know that, according to the latest and most authentic evidence, the Indian population of North America is, in some districts at least, not less numerous than it was two centuries ago, while its condition is greatly ameliorated.

Penn and Pennsylvania.

Penn and Pennsylvania.

THE history of Pennsylvania is remarkable for the exemption of the colony from those disasters which usually attend the infancy of such projects, and for the perpetuation of the most friendly relations between the settlers and the aborigines. These happy results were mainly due to the wise head and loving heart of the man who directed the enterprise—William Penn. Trained in the college, the camp, and the court; a student of men as well as of books, with sympathies and experience enlarged by foreign travel; full of a religious enthusiasm which suffering had deepened and purified, and which persecution had taught him to combine with a kindly tolerance for others, Penn was peculiarly fitted for the great work to which he devoted himself. His father, Admiral Penn, a brave but worldly-minded man, had ingratiated himself with King Charles II., by his offers, during the interregnum, to betray the Commonwealth, and by his subsequent services against the Dutch in 1665. Vain and ambitious, the old admiral desired to gratify those feelings by securing honours and advancement, not for himself, but for his son. He exerted himself to multiply and develop his estates, in order that his son might enjoy the revenues. He obtained the promise of a peerage from the king only in order that he might found a noble family. All his hopes were thus bound up in the future of his eldest son, and in the plans he had formed for his benefit. William Penn seemed likely to fulfil his father's aspirations. Of a comely presence, ready wit, and prepossessing manners, he bade fair by his own merits to second the admiral's influence. Just then the sect of Quakers was rising into notice. George Fox, the Nottingham shoemaker, had raised a crusade against steeple-churches, hireling ministers, and the recognition of different orders of men. This protest of the "man in the leather breeches," exaggerated and absurd in many respects, was only the natural reaction against the corruption and worldliness of the times, and elicited much sympathy among pious and earnest people. Young Penn, disgusted with the licentious and frivolous ways of his companions at Oxford, where he was now studying, had already begun to dream of pure and happy Utopia in that grand New World which he had heard his father and other travellers describe. The preaching of Thomas Loe, one of the disciples of George Fox, made such an impression on him that he joined the nonconformists who were then agitating the university, and was fined, and afterwards expelled for this conduct. His expulsion was a severe blow to his father's pride. William was coldly received at home, and quickly despatched on a foreign tour, in order to be cured of his nonconformist views. He was furnished with introductions to the highest circles, and amid the novel and impressive scenes and brilliant society of France and Italy, he soon forgot his recent austerity of demeanour. He returned from the Continent a dashing young gallant, who could wield a rapier, turn a compliment, or figure in a minuet with courtly ease and grace. His father was delighted with the change in his son's manners; but his delight was not of long continuance. It was at this time that the plague fell upon London, when men dropped down lifeless in the streets, and ten thousand deaths were reported in one day. Such an awful visitation was enough to awaken religious emotions even in the most thoughtless and indifferent mind, and it did not fail to revive the pious enthusiasm of William Penn. The admiral was absent on service against the Dutch, and on his return was surprised and mortified at his son's relapse into what he deemed a morbid and irrational melancholy. Again he endeavoured to restore his former gaiety by a change of scene. He sent him to the court of the Irish Viceroy, where he took a fancy to soldiering, and acquired some experience in military affairs, although he never entered the army. At Cork, William Penn again heard his old friend Loe, the itinerant Quaker, preach of the faith which "overcomes the world." From that moment he was possessed with "a deep sense of the vanity of the world, and the irreligiousness of its religions," which no amount of scorn or contumely, neither the persecutions of the law nor the threats and upbraidings of his father could unsettle. When he refused to doff his hat, even to his father or the king, the admiral in a rage turned him out of doors. He was sent to the Tower for heresy, and menaced with imprisonment for life unless he would recant. Brought to trial for having spoken at a Quaker meeting, the jury refused to convict him. Although reviled by the judge, and locked up without food or water for two days, the jurors adhered to their verdict. The court fined them for contumacy. Such was trial by jury in those days!

It was not long before father and son were reconciled. Before his death, which took place soon after, the admiral owned that he had spent his life in aiming after worthless things, and almost accepted the views of his Quaker son. Although inheriting an ample fortune, and mated with a lovely and accomplished wife, Penn did not abandon the unpopular cause with which he had identified himself. He was again imprisoned for several months, and on his release travelled with George Fox and other Quakers to preach the gospel to the Dutch and Germans, on whom they produced a deep impression.

The great idea of Penn's life was now approaching its consummation. George Fox had just returned from a visit to America. Travelling across the "great bogs" of the Dismal Swamp, and "commonly laying abroad o'nights in the woods by a fire," Fox had reached North Carolina, and received a warm welcome from the inhabitants. His description of these simple, honest exiles from the busy world, "hermits with wives and children," living in close communion with nature and in a state of freedom, and controlled only by conscience and reason, revived Penn's youthful dream of a free and virtuous state in the New World. Of all classes of nonconformists, the Quakers were most cruelly and unjustly used. They were hated not only by the Church and the King, but by the other dissenters and by the Protector. New England vied with old England in scourging them. Everywhere persecution followed them. For weary years they were whipped, pilloried, cast to rot in loathsome dungeons, mutilated, and not unfrequently hanged. As no other community could be found to tolerate them, it became absolutely necessary that they should create one of their own. Penn had taken a deep interest in the migration of a body of Quakers to New Jersey, and he now resolved to found a colony himself. He obtained a grant of land on the north bank of the Delaware, in liquidation of a debt of £16,000 which the Government owed his father. The province thus acquired contained no less than 47,000 square miles, being nearly as large as England. But it was as yet a wilderness, covered for the most part with tangled forests, and dotted only at rare intervals with the wigwams of an Indian camp or the solitary hut of wood and thatch of some Dutch or Swedish emigrant. A bare mountain chain intersected the country. Although the soil did not possess the spontaneous fertility of Virginia, it was capable of fruitful cultivation. The woods abounded with game and the rivers with fish.

Penn's last visit to the court was characteristic. When he received his charter from the hands of the king he observed his majesty take off his hat. "Friend Charles," he asked, "why dost thou not keep thy hat on thy head?" "Oh," replied the king, good-humouredly, "it is the custom, friend, in this place for only one person to remain covered at a time." It was on the 1st of September 1682 that Penn sailed for his new realm. He left behind his wife and children, in order to spare them the privations of an infant settlement. He gave them his counsel in a touching letter. His means being much reduced through his efforts for the public good, he reminded his wife of the necessity of economy, but at the same time desired her to be liberal in the education of their children. Looking forward to the time when they would join him in the colony, he was anxious that the two boys should acquire a sound knowledge of building, ship-carpentry, surveying, navigation, and especially agriculture, and that Letty should learn to manage a household. "Let my children," he said, "be husbandmen and housewives." On the 27th of October, after a melancholy voyage, during which the small-pox carried off thirty of the hundred passengers, Penn first set foot on the New World, at Newcastle. On the following day, in the presence of a crowd of emigrants who had preceded him, he received possession of the land by the typical delivery of a lump of earth and a cup of water. Ascending the stately stream of the Delaware to Upland (afterwards named Chester), then the chief place in the province, he convoked a parliament, who in three days adopted a constitution passed a number of laws, and then returned to their ploughs and oxen. The constitution secured freedom of thought, sacredness of person and property, and popular control over all the powers of the state. It recognised the right of every child to instruction, and of every adult to a vote. Penn's next duty was to choose a site for and prepare the plan of a metropolis. He would not allow the capital of his dominions to grow up as accident or caprice might direct. With characteristic foresight he designed it from the first with an eye to its future greatness. Two noble streets were to front the river. The High Street was to be a magnificent avenue, one hundred feet wide, bordered with trees and beds of flowers. Disliking the closely packed towns of the Old World, he desired that gardens might be mingled with the streets, so as to form a "greene country town."

Before, however, a single house could be erected, a throng of emigrants arrived, not only from England but from Holland, Germany, and Sweden, and other parts to which the news had spread that William Penn, the Quaker, had opened "an asylum for the good and oppressed of every nation." In the absence of houses, they took shelter in the large caves which were to be found on the banks of the Delaware. Their sufferings must have been severe, but they bore them with patience and fortitude. "Delicate women, used to all the luxuries of the earth in England, went out to help their fathers and husbands: they brought in the wood and water; they cooked the victuals with their own hands; they tended sheep and pigs, game and poultry; some of them acted as labourers while the house was building, anxious to carry mortar or lend a hand to saw a block of wood, as the case required. If a murmur once arose, the thought of that 'woful Europe' which they had left behind soon checked it, and all worked on cheerily."*

The first building completed was used as a tavern, exchange, and ferry-house. But others soon followed. In August 1683, save three or four little cabins, the only dwellings were the caves by the river-side,

* Dixon's "Life of Penn."

hollow trees, or temporary tents. The deer browsed on their accustomed pastures, and the conies disported round their ancient burrows. If a stranger ventured but a little way from the river he was lost in the mazes of a dense forest. But within a few months after the foundation of the city, eighty houses and cottages were ready. One year after Penn landed, a hundred houses had been built, the whole plan of the city had been laid out, sixty vessels had arrived in the Delaware, and more than three hundred farms had been settled. Before another year was over the place contained about six hundred houses, and the school-master and the printing-press had begun their work. With just exultation might the leader of this great enterprise write to his friends, "I must without vanity say I have led the greatest colony into America that ever man did on private credit."

But it was in his treatment of the natives that Penn's character was most nobly displayed. With fervent faith in the inherent virtues of the Indians, he would not allow his followers to arm themselves even in self-defence. He believed that the best way to overcome the suspicion of the red men was to repose implicit confidence in their honour and humanity. Before he left England he addressed a letter to them, in which he declared that he and they shared a common responsibility to one God, and were alike bound to love, help, and do good to one another. To Colonel Markham, his deputy, he gave strict injunctions not to take an inch of ground from the Indians without meeting their just demands. When he himself reached the colony one of his first cares was to assemble the chiefs of the tribes, in order to ratify the bargains which had been made in his name.

This conclave was held at Shakamaxon, on the northern edge of Philadelphia. A majestic elm, already one hundred and fifty-five years old, rose in the midst of a sort of natural amphitheatre, which had from time immemorial formed the meeting-place of the tribes, when they lighted the council fire or smoked the calumet of peace. The Indian sachems, men of imposing mien and grave demeanour, decked in their holiday garb, sat upon the ground, in the form of a half-moon—the old men being in the front row, and the middle-aged men in a second row at a little distance behind them. The young foresters were grouped in a third semi-circle in the rear. None of the Indians carried arms, and the oldest of the sachems wore on his forehead the mystic horn which rendered the spot sacred and the persons of all present inviolable. The English also appeared unarmed. They clustered, without distinction of rank, round the old elm,—a motley throng of grave English nonconformists, grim old soldiers of Gustavus Adolphus, Dutchmen and Germans. In the centre stood William Penn, undistinguished in attire from his companions except by a silken sash round his waist. He was then in the prime of manhood,—

"one of the handsomest, best looking, and lively gentlemen," said a lady who was present at this great ceremony. There was nothing of the Quaker in his appearance. Although simple, his dress was handsome, and his long auburn hair fell in rich clusters from beneath his slouched hat.

When all had taken their places, Penn propounded the treaty of peace and friendship which he desired to form with the Indians:—They were each to respect the pursuits and possessions of the other; and any difference between them was to be settled by a jury, composed of so many men of each race. "We meet," said Penn, "on the broad pathway of good faith and good will: no advantage shall be taken on either side, but all shall be openness and love. I will not call you children, for parents sometimes chide their children too severely; nor brothers only, for brothers differ. We are the same as if one man's body were to be divided into two parts; we are all one flesh and blood."

The Indian king responded with grave enthusiasm. "We will live," they said to the English, as they delivered the belt of wampum,* "in love with Mr. Penn and his children as long as the sun and moon shall endure. We will have a broad path for you

---

* Wampum, or wampum peag (as it is properly called), was formed from a peculiar kind of shell. Of this substance there were two kinds, black and white. The black peag consisted of a small round spot on the inside of a shell, which was cut out, polished, and strung on a thread. The wampum peag (white sort) was the twisted end of several small shells broken off from the main part. These were also strung on threads, and worn as bracelets, necklaces, and belts. Belts of wampum were

and us to walk in. If an Englishman fall asleep in this path, the Indian shall pass him by, and say, 'He is an Englishman; he is asleep; let him alone.' The path shall be plain; there shall not be a stump in it to hurt the feet."

These words were sincere, and were never forgotten. The simple sons of the forest, says the historian of America, returning to their wigwams, kept the history of the covenant by strings of wampum; and long afterwards in their cabins would count over the shells on a clean piece of bark, and recall to their own memory, and repeat to their children or the stranger, the words of Mr. Penn. It is a remarkable fact that not a drop of Quaker blood was ever shed by the Indians; and that when, forty years after the death of Penn, an Indian was slain by a Pennsylvanian, the countrymen of the victim begged that his life might be spared. He died, however, soon after, and then they said the Great Spirit was avenged.

During the whole of his stay in the colony Penn remained on the most affectionate terms with the natives. He visited their camp, learned several of their dialects, walked with them alone in the forest, shared their homely feasts of hominy and roasted acorns,

---

often exchanged at the negotiation of treaties, and were on such occasions so contrived as to be a record of the agreement. When used as currency between the English and natives, six of the white, or three of the black beads were valued at an English penny, and a fathom length came to about five shillings. In 1645 a fine of two thousand fathoms of wampum was imposed by the English on the Narragansetts at the close of the war, which it took them five years to pay up.

PENN'S TREATY WITH THE INDIANS.

Page 107.

and even joined in their athletic games. At a leaping match one day he entered the ring and distanced all the young men, to their surprise and admiration.

Of the administration of the colony it is not necessary to speak in detail. Its spirit and general character may be gathered from the fact that an appeal to a council of peace-makers was directed to precede any trial in a court of law, and that a court was appointed to take care of widows and orphans. Enlightened as was Penn's policy towards the Indians, he was but little in advance of his contemporaries in his views as to the negroes. He shared the general belief that they were an inferior race, destined to serve the more intellectual nations. But if at first he held their bondage to be justifiable, he exerted himself to raise the moral condition of the slaves, and, towards the close of his life, condemned the whole system.

Based on such sound principles, and favoured by such a happy inauguration, the colony, as was to be expected, enjoyed a growing and stable prosperity. Very diffcrent was the fate of its magnanimous founder. Returning to England to look after his affairs, the favour which James II. had shown him caused him to be suspected. After the Revolution jealous and interested rivals did their best to blacken his character. He was several times arrested, and each time acquitted. Engrossed with the welfare of humanity, he allowed his estates to be ravaged by a roguish steward, who involved him in difficulties, which he turned to his own profit. Broken in fortune, he applied to the colonists for a loan of £10,000, but they ungratefully evaded his request. Not content with denying him assistance, they even sought to encroach upon his proprietary rights within the province. On his return to Pennsylvania, however, before the close of the century, a reconciliation was effected between him and his people. The few years which he spent at Pennsbury—a manor-house in the old English style, which he built on his colonial domain—were the happiest he was destined to enjoy. Recalled to England again by new intrigues against him at court, his declining years were imbittered by a succession of troubles and disappointments. He died in 1718.

It does not fall within the scope of this little volume to describe the foundation of each of the American colonies; but the following extract from one of Mr. Everett's lectures will illustrate the general character of the leading settlements:—

"The first settlement, that of Virginia, was commenced in the spirit of worldly enterprise, with no slight dash, however, of chivalry and romance on the part of its leader. In the next generation this colony became the favourite resort of the loyal cavaliers and gentlemen who were disgusted by the austerities of the English Commonwealth, or fell under its suspicion. In the meantime, New England was founded by those who suffered the penalties of nonconformity. The mighty change of 1640 stopped the tide of emigration to New England, but recruited Virginia with those who were disaffected to Cromwell. In 1624 the island of Manhattan was purchased of the Indians for twenty-four dollars;—a sum of money, by the way, which seems rather low for 22,000 acres of land, including the site of a great metropolis, but which would, if put out at compound interest at 7 per cent in 1624, not perhaps fall so very much below even its present value. Maryland next attracted those who adhered to the Roman Catholic faith. New Jersey and Pennsylvania were mainly settled by persecuted Quakers; but the latter offered an asylum to the Germans whom the sword of Louis XIV. drove from the Palatinate. The French Huguenots, driven out by the revocation of the Edict of Nantes, scattered themselves from Massachusetts to Carolina. The Dutch and Swedish settlements on the Hudson and the Delaware provided a kindred home for such of their countrymen as desired to try the fortune of the New World. The Whigs of England, who rebelled against James II. in 1685, and were sent to the Transatlantic colonies, lived long enough to meet in exile the adherents of his son, who rebelled against George I. in 1715. The oppressed Protestants of Salzburg came with General Oglethorpe to Georgia; and the

Highlanders who fought for Charles Edward in 1745, were deported by hundreds to North Carolina. They were punished by being sent from their bleak hills and sterile moors to a land of abundance and liberty; they were banished from oatmeal porridge to meat twice a day. The Gaelic language is still spoken by their descendants."

The Scottish Colony of Darien.

I.—WILLIAM PATERSON.
II.—THE FIRST EXPEDITION.
III.—THE DISASTERS AT DARIEN.

The Scottish Colony of Darien.

I.—WILLIAM PATERSON.

ON the south side of Edinburgh, not far from the new Industrial Museum, might be seen, until recently, an old-fashioned building, whose high-pitched roof, and walls pierced with niches, bore testimony to its former estate. Attached to its weather-stained front was a tablet bearing the date 1698, marking the memorable period in Scottish history when the enterprise represented by those four grim walls was the pride and hope of the nation. For that edifice was the remnant of the old Darien House, the seat of the great Company whose coffers received almost the entire available capital of Scotland, and was to regenerate the social condition of the country, by developing a wide and lucrative commerce. We cannot but regret its removal as a memorial of the past, though it belonged to a time when England and Scotland were not united, as they now are, in the bonds of peace and concord.

It was in 1695 that the scheme for the establishment of a Scottish colony on the shores of Darien was first published. It was conceived in 1684, by William Paterson, the eminent merchant who designed and helped to found the Bank of England. It is strange that the personal career of a man who, by his connection with such schemes, left so deep an impress on his times, should be shrouded in oblivion; yet such is the case. He stands before us little more than the shadow of a great name. Of his birth, the date was 1658; and the place somewhere in Dumfries-shire—tradition pointing to Tinwald. Having espoused the cause of the Covenanters, he was obliged at an early age to seek safety by quitting his native country. He spent a number of years in mercantile pursuits in the West Indies. Returning to London, he brought forward his plan for a national bank in 1691, but had to wait several years before it was taken up by the Government. In that institution, when started (1693), he was a shareholder to the extent of £2000, and took his seat among the first Directors. In the course of a year, however, he was quietly elbowed out of the concern. The portrait of Paterson fully confirms the impression of his character which is created by all we know about him. We look upon a thoughtful, earnest face, kindly in its glance, yet sad withal; a broad, full forehead; clear, open eyes; and firm-set nostrils, which seem somewhat at issue with a chin of weaker mould. The picture, which was found in an old volume, bears the inscription, "*Sic vos non vobis;*" —which was truly the legend of his life.

After the establishment of the Bank of England, Paterson continued in business as a merchant; but the mere pursuit of individual gain was not sufficient to satisfy his aspirations. His mind now recurred to his experiences in the West Indies.

Of a humane and philanthropic nature, he deplored the lawless lives and horrible excesses of the freebooters; and with his shrewd eye at once detected the cause of the disorder, and foresaw the only effectual remedy. The terrible Brotherhood of the coast sprang from the unnatural exclusiveness of the Spaniards, as directly as filth breeds vermin, and corruption worms. "No peace beyond the line," was the obvious reply to "No faith with heretics," and "No trade with foreigners." The selfish monopoly which Spain tried to enforce in regard to America was as unjustifiable as it was absurd. Not only the settlement, but the visit of all foreigners was prohibited with more than Japanese severity. No stranger could set foot on any portion of the immense territory claimed by Spain under penalty of death. Even Spaniards were not allowed to visit their own colonies, except by royal license, and for a brief period. Paterson saw clearly that the only way to get rid of piracy in the Spanish main was to open a channel for legitimate commerce, and to enlist the enterprise and daring of such men as Morgan and Dampier in a peaceful course. A free settlement would secure that object.

As a site for such a settlement, he fixed upon the Isthmus of Darien. That narrow neck of land, which links together the two great continents of America, by its very appearance suggests the idea of a communication, across its slender waist, between the Pacific and Atlantic Oceans, which would enable vessels not only to escape the furies which guard the routes round Cape Horn and the Cape of Good Hope, but to pass more speedily from the one side of the world to the other. Paterson saw, further, that a passage from Europe to Asia *via* Panama would enable vessels to avail themselves of the tradewinds, which would be always in their favour. It is doubtful whether Paterson himself ever visited the Isthmus before he accompanied the colony thither; but he collected a vast amount of information respecting it from Dampier, the buccaneer captain, who had crossed it with his men; Wafer, the surgeon, who had resided for some time among the natives; and many others who had been on the spot. He learned that, narrow as is the neck of land, the journey from one shore to the other is impeded by forbidding heights, dense forests, tangled brakes, and pestilential swamps; but he was told, also, that in spite of these obstacles the journey had been accomplished in three days, and that the natives were able to do it in half the time.

It was not till this scheme had been rejected by the English Government, and one of the German princes, to whom he submitted it, that it occurred to him to propose it to his native country. This idea was encouraged by Fletcher of Saltoun, whom he met in London. Lord Macaulay's eloquent pen does justice to the magnificent speculations of the two friends: "Of the kingdoms of Europe, Scotland was, as yet, the poorest and the least considered. If she would but occupy Darien; if she would but become one great free port, one great warehouse for the wealth which the soil of Darien might produce, and for the still greater wealth which would be poured into Darien from Canton and Siam, from Ceylon and the Moluccas, from the mouths of the Ganges and the Gulf of Cambay,—she would at once take her place in the first rank among nations. No rival would be able to contend with her either in the West Indian or in the East Indian trade. The beggarly country, as it had been insolently called by the inhabitants of warmer and more fruitful regions, would be the great mart for the choicest luxuries,—sugar, rum, coffee, chocolate, tobacco, the tea and porcelain of China, the muslin of Dacca, the shawls of Cashmere, the diamonds of Golconda, the pearls of Karrack, the delicious birds' nests of Nicobar, cinnamon and pepper, ivory and sandal-wood. From Scotland would come all the finest jewels and brocade worn by duchesses at the balls of St. James's and

Versailles. From Scotland would come all the saltpetre which would furnish the means of war to the fleets and armies of contending potentates. And on all the vast riches which would be constantly passing through the little kingdom a toll would be paid, which would remain behind. There would be a prosperity such as might seem fabulous—a prosperity of which every Scotchman, from the peer to the cadie, would partake. Soon, all along the now desolate shores of the Forth and Clyde, villas and pleasure-grounds would be as thick as along the edges of the Dutch canals. Edinburgh would vie with London and Paris; and the bailie of Glasgow or Dundee would have as stately and well-furnished a mansion, and as fine a gallery of pictures, as any burgomaster of Amsterdam."

II.—THE FIRST EXPEDITION.

It is probable that King William and his ministers never dreamed, when they assented to the Act for establishing what was afterwards known as the Darien Company, that Scotland would be able to carry it out. It would serve, they thought, as a useful stalking horse to divert attention from the Glencoe Massacre, and when that object had been attained it would fall to pieces of its own accord. Those who argued thus little understood the mood in which Scotland took up the scheme. The Scotch were tired of barren wars. They were anxious to develop the resources of the country, which had hitherto been wasted by misgovernment and chronic revolution, and to devote to peaceful industry that energy and enterprise which they had displayed on the field and in the foray. Paterson, in proposing the colonization of Darien, only gave a direction and supplied a form to a spirit which already pervaded the nation. Never was the *perfervidum ingenium Scotorum* thrown so hotly and heartily into any project. The people hastened to enter their names on the subscription list as eagerly as they signed the Solemn League and Covenant; and carried out the enterprise with all the ardour and enthusiasm with which they had formerly rabbled the English clergy, or braved Cromwell and his Ironsides.

It was originally intended to raise half of the capital in England, and shares were readily taken there. Some of the southern merchants, however, raised an outcry against the scheme. They declared that the Isthmus belonged to Spain, and that any attempt to land there would lead to a war, of which England would have to bear the brunt. The truth is, that the title of Spain to the Isthmus was worthless. It was founded on an idle bull of Pope Alexander VI., in the sixteenth century, which divided the undiscovered countries of the world between the Spaniards and the Portuguese by a line drawn one hundred leagues west of the Azores, and which had always been scouted by England, while but little regard had been paid to it even by Roman Catholic powers. Moreover, the title was not supported by occupation, for of the Spanish stations in that quarter the nearest was more than one hundred miles from Caledonia Bay.

As to the capacity of the Scots to defend their settlement, without aid from England, against the Spaniards, it was notorious—such was the prostration and decrepitude of that power at the time—that twelve hundred men bred, as most of the colonists were, to arms, could have marched from one end of South America to the other and plundered almost every Spanish station they came to, without meeting any formidable resistance. The real secret of the English opposition was the alarm lest Scotland should gain any share of the English trade. In consequence of the clamour which was raised, the Company was forbidden to receive any money in England; and the King even went so far as to dictate to the merchants of Hamburgh not to support the scheme,—an interference which was resented by the Senate of that city, but did not fail to check the subscriptions.*

Notwithstanding these discouragements, the Darien Company resolved to go on with its preparations.

* The most conclusive and damnatory proof of the treachery of the English Government towards the Scots' Colony is to be found in the journals of the Board of Trade, which show that at the very time when they were denouncing the Company for invading the rights of Spain, the Board had reported that Spain had no claim to the central district of Darien, that it formed an admirable site for a settlement, and that a body of men should be sent with despatch to anticipate the Scots in taking possession of it

Its operations were not confined to the founding of a colony, but included the development of Scottish fisheries and manufactures, and the establishment of trade with Africa and Russia.

In the summer of 1698 the first expedition to Darien was got ready. It was on a sunny day in July that the first fleet of three vessels, with twelve hundred picked men, sailed from Leith, amidst the cheers of a vast multitude assembled on the beach; among whom were numbers who were so anxious to accompany the expedition that they clung to the sides of the vessels as they were weighing anchor, and were only plucked away by main force. On the 30th October the emigrants came in sight of the New World, and two days afterwards reached Golden Island, which had been named as the destination of the expedition. Their first glimpse of their new home delighted them. Golden Island lay at the entrance of a wide bay, fringed with golden sands, and interspersed with dark mangrove beds. The shores were crowned with groves of stately trees, and backed by a fine range of wooded hills. A narrow strait gave access to the bay, which once entered was safe and commodious. On a peninsula edged with rock, which formed one of the jaws of the harbour, the Scots fixed their fort, cutting through the narrow neck which united it to the mainland, in order to form an island. In this "crabbed hold" they took up their abode. The first day was spent in pitching tents and exploring the locality. The emigrants were pleased with the abundance of game which they started in the woods, and with the shoals of fish which they saw darting about in the crystal waters. The season was peculiarly genial. Palm trees mingled their broad leaves to form thick screens, which offered a pleasant shade; graceful cocoa-nuts and cassavas waved overhead; tufts of bamboo were interspersed with heavy trees, whose branches supported gigantic orchids, and whose stems were concealed amid a mass of purple convolvuli and other brilliant climbers. No time was lost in erecting fortifications, and mounting guns. Rude huts were also built of precious woods, which in Europe form the ornament of palaces.

Immediately on their arrival the Scots had been visited by a party of natives, with whom the Council had made terms for a settlement. The king of the country lived further inland; and Paterson and some others went to pay their respects to him. Their first impressions of the fertility of the Isthmus were confirmed by this journey. Maize, bananas, and pine-apples were found in profusion. As they approached the royal court, they were met by a body of musicians playing on reeds, and attended by a crowd of people, who raised a "loud humming" chorus. The king, who wore a diadem of gold, and a light cotton robe, received them graciously, twirling his nose-ring, as " white men sometimes twirl their mustachios." The priests were asked to disclose the character and designs of the white strangers. As they were engaged in the mysteries of divination, a loud chattering was heard, the branches of the trees became violently agitated, and a large troop of monkeys suddenly appeared upon the scene. They were hailed with delight by the priests, who declared that it was a happy omen. A treaty was thereupon made between the Indians and the Scots, and peace declared " as long as rivers ran, and gold was found in Darien ;" which was the native expression, says the chronicle, for eternity.

III.—THE DISASTERS AT DARIEN.

In those days colonization was in its infancy; and Scotland was especially inexperienced in the art. Many blunders were made in fitting out the Darien expedition; and the settlers were, of course, not exempt from those troubles and dangers which beset every young colony. At all times a draught of the home population to a distant part of the earth must include a large number of restless, unsettled men, who are anxious to exchange the discipline of cities for the license of the wilds. Among the Scotch emigrants was a knot of "mean spirits, raw heads, jealous and presumptuous pates," who introduced the leaven of discord into the little community. Unfortunately, the constitution of the colony provided no check upon this faction. The Council of Seven, which had been appointed by the Company, distracted by mutual jealousy and distrust, would not elect a president for more than a week; and each new president, of course, undid the work of his predecessor. The stores with which the Company had loaded the ships were ill-selected, and of inferior quality. The provisions were especially bad, and had not been improved by the sea-voyage. A portion of them had to be cast into the sea. The rod and the gun, however, supplied the settlers with fish and game; and the Indians daily visited the camp with yams, plantains, and cocoa-nuts, which they sold for a handful of beads, or a few trinkets. Although they were still in the "dry" season of the year, the weather had been wet and boisterous, and had somewhat retarded the work of clearing and building. Idleness fomented strife. The internal disorder might have proved fatal to the colony, had not a counter-irritant diverted the bad humours and restored harmony.

In the beginning of 1699 rumours reached the ears of the Scots that the Spaniards were mustering a powerful force to oust them from their settlement. There does not appear to have been any foundation for these reports; but they had the good effect of quelling domestic quarrels, and of leading the various factions, with one consent, to join in hurrying on the fortifications. In March, the *Dolphin*, a sloop of fourteen guns, was wrecked in a storm upon the beach of Carthagena. The crew were seized by the Spaniards, and treated as slaves. When the news of this outrage reached Fort St. Andrew, an envoy with a flag of truce was at once despatched, to demand the release of the prisoners and indemnity for the insult, under a threat of instant reprisals. The governor of Carthagena received the message in a furious passion, tore up a copy of the Company's charter which had been sent for his inspection, called the Scots "rogues and pirates," and was with difficulty persuaded to respect the sacred character of the envoy. The Council of Caledonia, in great indignation, instantly issued letters of mark and reprisal.

Busied with preparations against the Spaniards, the emigrants had no time to grumble over their food, or to quarrel with each other. In spite of the rumoured approach of the enemy, the colony was tranquil and hopeful. And indeed they had, as they knew, but little to fear from that quarter. The Spaniards were notoriously weak, and Fort St. Andrew was impregnable to arms.

On the 9th April a singular proclamation was issued by the governors of Jamaica, Barbadoes, and New York, in obedience to instructions from England, repudiating all connection with the Scots, and prohibiting the English colonists, under heavy penalties, from giving them " any assistance in

arms, ammunition, or any other necessity whatever."*
The little band of Scots reeled under the shock of
this ruthless proclamation, which amounted to a sentence of death by starvation. They might make head
against the Spaniards;—they could not cope with
the treacherous and implacable foe whom they had
found in their own sovereign. In their rocky stronghold they could withstand any enemy save one, and
that was famine, which now stared them in the face.
Their stores were well-nigh exhausted, and there was
no sign of supplies from Scotland. The vessel they
had sent to Jamaica for food had returned empty.
For a time "the generous savages, by hunting and
fishing for them, gave them that relief which fellow
Britons refused;" but the rainy season, of which they
had had but a slight foretaste, now commenced in
earnest, and the natives withdrew to the interior. The
rain descended in ceaseless torrents. The heat increased. The atmosphere became close and suffocating.
Swarms of noxious vermin filled the air and covered
the ground. From the black, slimy mangrove
swamps along the shore the pestilence might be seen
steaming up in a dense vapour. With bodies enfeebled by want, and hearts sick with hope deferred,

---

* In North America and the West Indies the most savage pirates and buccaneers, men who might be termed enemies of the human race, and had done deeds which seemed to exclude them from intercourse with mankind, had, nevertheless, found repeated refuge,—had been permitted to refit their squadrons, and supplied with every means of keeping the sea, had set sail in a condition to commit new murders and piracies. But no such relief was extended to the Scots, acting under a charter from their sovereign, and establishing a peaceful colony according to the law of nations, and for the universal benefit of mankind.—*Sir Walter Scott.*

the emigrants fell an easy prey to the maladies of the season, which, in good health and spirits, they might have resisted. The deaths rose to ten and twelve a day. Those who were equal to the exertion dragged their feeble, wasted limbs, to the hill behind the settlement, where they sat, and with wild, blood-shot eyes, scanned the ocean in the hope of seeing it flecked with the white sails of the long expected ship. Paterson strove to cheer up his companions, and besought them to hold on for a little longer, confident that the Company would not abandon them. Every day the cry became stronger and more desperate—"Let us flee while yet we have life." Paterson himself had buried his wife, the only woman who accompanied the expedition, and was now stricken by the fever. Eight months had been spent in the Isthmus, and not a word of encouragement, not a morsel of provisions had arrived from Scotland. On the 9th of June the emigrants embarked on board of three ships, and set sail for "the first port to which it pleased Providence to send them." Hundreds perished at sea. A storm separated the fleet. Two of the vessels reached New York, and the sight of the miserable skeletons on board moved the authorities to disregard the proclamation, and to allow them to procure food, and to refit their shattered barks. The third vessel arrived at Jamaica, where, but for the secret charity of some private persons, they would have died on the beach from utter want.

When the tidings of these disasters reached Scotland, the nation was at first incredulous. When it was found that they were only too true, there was a burst of scorn and indignation at the cowardice of the deserters. There had been a dearth in Scotland, and the Company, in the belief that the colonists had sufficient supplies, had not deemed it necessary to forward more within so short a period. But in May 1699 they despatched a couple of vessels with provisions. In August other four vessels, with thirteen hundred men, sailed, amidst the blessings of the nation. These reinforcements arrived at Darien to find the fort in ruins, and the huts a heap of charred embers. The rapid growth of tropical vegetation had overrun the settlement, and almost effaced the traces of the hand of man. "The site marked out for the proud capital, which was to have been the Tyre, the Venice, the Amsterdam of the eighteenth century, was overgrown with jungle, and inhabited only by the sloth and the baboon." No wonder the hearts of the adventurers sank within them. Gradually a few of the deserters came back, and another expedition, consisting of three hundred men, under Campbell of Finab—a soldier of tried courage and ability—reached Darien. But the Scots had no heart to recommence the clearance of the ground, or to rebuild the little town. Self-defence led them to repair the fortifications, but they dwelt chiefly on board of their vessels. Feuds broke out among the idle and disappointed men. An apprehension spread among the weaker and more quiet portion of the band that the others intended to seize them and sell them into slavery in the French and Spanish plantations. Provisions were scanty and bad; and, as if no element of discord should be wanting, the four clergymen who accompanied the expedition estranged the good-will of their flock by holding daily services of three and even six hours in length, and denouncing as children of the Evil One all who showed irritation under that irksome dispensation.

The Spaniards, encouraged by the policy of England, were now active in their hostility to the colony. When Campbell of Finab heard a rumour of their approach, he resolved to anticipate them. On the 5th February 1700 he set out, at the head of two hundred Scots, to cross the Isthmus. On the third day they descended the mountains towards "the pleasant south sea." The Spaniards were garrisoned at a fort named Tubucanti. Campbell was ignorant of the numbers of the garrison, but conceived that his duty bade him assail it. The Spaniards fled in alarm at such an intrepid movement, and among the spoils which the Scots carried back in triumph was the golden fleece of the Spanish general. On their return to Caledonia, their exultation over this victory was changed to dismay by the sight of five men-of-war blockading the harbour. An open fight was out of the question, but they held out for six weeks. By that time many of the chief men of the expedition were dead. The enemy had cut off the wells, and were every day drawing nearer. All the pewter dishes in the fort had been melted into cannon balls. Inevitable famine compelled the colonists to an honourable surrender; but they were so few, and feeble from exhaustion, that, but for the assistance of the Spaniards, they could not have weighed the anchor of their vessel. Campbell of Finab refused to be included in the terms of capitulation, but escaped in the night, and returned to Scotland in safety.

Thus ended the ill-starred attempt of the Scots to plant a colony in Darien. The rage and mortification of the nation at the overthrow of its magnificent design knew no bounds, and for a time a rebellion against King William, who was regarded as the author of the mischief, appeared inevitable. Paterson, who had conceived the plan of the colony, helped to heal the breach between the two nations by advocating the Union, under the terms of which indemnification was awarded to the Scots for their losses in the Darien expedition. Paterson had lost everything in the adventure. He had spent many years and £10,000 in establishing the Company. He had been awarded a handsome per centage on the stock and profits of the undertaking; but before the first expedition sailed he had generously abandoned his claim. After the Union, a Royal Commission recommended that he should receive £18,000, as a return for his services and losses; but it is doubtful whether more than a fragment of the sum was paid to him. He represented Dumfries in the first united Parliament, and was well known at his death as an able financier.

Dominion of Canada.

I.—CANADA.
II.—RUPERT'S LAND AND THE RED RIVER TERRITORY.
III.—VANCOUVER'S ISLAND AND BRITISH COLUMBIA.

Dominion of Canada.

I.—CANADA.

"THE French," justly observes Mr. Everett in one of his essays, "although excelling all other nations in the art of communicating for temporary purposes with savage tribes, seem still more than the Spaniards to be destitute of the august skill required to found new states. Half a million of French peasants in Lower Canada, tenaciously adhering to the manners and customs which their fathers brought from Normandy two centuries ago, and a third part of that number of planters of French descent in Louisiana, are all that is left to bear witness to the amazing fact, that in the middle of the last century, France was the mistress of the better half of North America."—How that vast territory passed from her grasp, it is no part of our story to tell. Its loss was due partly to the fortunes of war, and partly to her own mismanagement. In 1759, Quebec was captured by General Wolfe, in that memorable siege in which he lost his life; and Canada was subsequently ceded in full to Great Britain by treaty in 1763. At that period the colonial population was almost exclusively French, and the various settlements were in a frail and languid state. The French lacked not the industry, but the steady perseverance, which was required to subdue the hard, illiberal soil, to a fruitful mood, and the tiresome labour of the axe disheartened them. Comparatively speaking, their clearings and tilled fields were but mere specks on the wide expanse of tangled forest. The seizure of Quebec by arms, however brilliant as a military exploit, was but a step towards the real conquest of Canada. The subjugation of her idle woods and barren wastes is a triumph of which we have still more reason to be proud. During the last quarter of a century the progress of the colony has been rapid and sustained. In 1838, Lord Durham described it as the home of "a widely scattered population, poor, and apparently unenterprising, though hardy and industrious; separated from each other by tracts of intervening forest; without towns and markets, almost without roads; living in mean houses, drawing little more than a rude subsistence from ill-cultivated land, and seemingly incapable of improving their condition."—Since then, a great change has come over the spirit of the people and the aspect of the land. Enterprise and energy now characterize the colonists. The forests have receded before the axe, and yellow harvests wave upon their former sites. Squalid Indian villages have given place to populous and flourishing towns; and an extensive railway system embraces the country.

The soil of Canada is remarkable for its fertility. In some parts it is said to be almost too rich for wheat, while in others it will yield crops of that grain for twenty or thirty years without manuring. In cereal produce, Canada may now be said to be unsurpassed by any country in the world. Her trees, however, form her especial glory. Enormous forests of maple, beech, oak, basswood, ash, elm, hickory, walnut, chestnut, cherry, birch, cedar, and pine, stretch far and wide over the country, and supply a precious mine of wealth. Some of these trees assume gigantic proportions. The white spruce attains a height of 140 feet, and the Weymouth pine, 200 feet. One of the latter has been known to exhibit 1500 annular divisions in its stem, thus proving it to be of great antiquity. A Scotch backwoodsman, Mr. Linton, counted the rings of an oak between Lake Huron and the head of Lake Ontario, and calculated that it had been a sapling in the days of Wallace and Bruce.

The "lumberer" has been the pioneer of Canadian colonization. Encamping in the heart of the forest, the "lumberer" plies the axe during the summer and autumn. Before the winter arrives, many a tall tree has been laid low in the dust. The frozen snow offers a smooth, firm pathway, over which horses drag the felled logs to the brink of the nearest stream. When the thaw comes, they are floated down into some navigable river, where they are made up into rafts, and steered, perhaps for hundreds of miles, to Quebec. The piloting of these huge rafts down the numerous rapids which they have to traverse demands a quick eye and strong nerve, and is not free from peril. The rafts consist of several portions called "bonds," each of which is subdivided into "cribs." When a cataract has to be descended, the whole "bond" goes down together; but when a "shoot" has been provided, in order to avoid a dangerous or impassable fall, each crib traverses it separately, and rejoins its associates below. Mr. Woods, in describing the "shoot," or canal on a slope, which the Prince of Wales descended with the Governor-General and the Duke of Newcastle, says:—"A certain portion of the river is dammed off, and turned into a broad wide channel of timber, which is taken at a sharp incline cut into the bank of the river, and down which, of course, the waters of the Ottawa rush at terrific speed. The head of this 'shoot' is placed some 300 or 400 yards above the falls, and terminates, after a run of about three-quarters of a mile, in the still waters of the river below their base. But a raft on such a steep incline, and hurried along by such a rush of water, would attain a speed which would destroy itself and all upon it. The fall of the shoot is broken at intervals by straight runs, along which it glides at a comparatively reduced speed, till it again dashes over the next incline, and commences another headlong rush. Some of these runs terminate with a perpendicular drop of three or four feet, over which the raft goes smack, and wallows in the boiling water beneath, till the current again gets the mastery, and forces it on faster and more furiously than before. More than 20,000,000 cubic feet of timber come down the shoots of the Ottawa in this manner each year."—During the journey, the lumberers, in their red jerseys, seated on their piles of yellow logs, form a picturesque sight.

The plough follows the axe. In the track of the lumberer comes the backwoods farmer. He finds the ground partially cleared, but by no means bare of trees; so he sets to work to complete the task. After felling the remaining trunks, and rooting up the stumps over an acre or so, he assembles his friends to what is called a "logging bee." In the backwoods, when labour is scarce, it is the fashion for settlers to give each other a day's work occasionally. From far and near, at daybreak, flock the neighbours, with their teams of stout oxen and strong iron chains, with which they drag away the felled trees. These are then piled in heaps, and burned. A homely but hearty feast closes the day of kindly labour. Before long, fields are enclosed and cultivated, and there are harvests to reap. Roads hitherto have been mere accidents. A broad thoroughfare would gradually narrow into a mere squirrel track, and finally, as the Yankees say, run up a tree. But with the increase of farms, and the growth of crops, regular highways become a necessity, and are accordingly constructed. In the course of time, houses spring up by the side of the most frequented roads, hamlets rise into villages, and villages swell into towns.

According to an official return issued a few years ago, Canada proper contains 350,000 square miles, of which only some 40,000 were then cleared. The large portion of this area, however, which lies to the north of the St. Lawrence, on the Labrador coast, does not offer a tempting prospect to the colonist. It is anticipated that before many years elapse, the whole of Western Canada will be settled, and that colonization will then tend in a north-easterly direction.

The two Canadas now comprise a population which is not far short of 3,000,000, or about as large as that of the thirteen States of America which in the last century withdrew their allegiance from Great Britain. The importance of the colony may be gathered from the fact, that its imports amount to about £8,000,000, and its exports to nearly £7,000,000. A vast system of inland navigation—the grandest in the world—extends from the ocean to the prairies of the Far West, through Canadian rivers, lakes, and canals. Immediate and direct water communication is thus afforded between the very heart of the country and its seaboard, embracing 2000 miles of inland coast, without referring to the nearly equal extent of coast belonging to the States, or the vast affluents which feed the St. Lawrence and the lakes. In not a few cases a vessel, built and loaded with a cargo in the backwoods, has traversed this great artery of commerce, has crossed the ocean, and, reaching England, has found a purchaser both for itself and its contents. In addition to this inland navigation, Canada has a magnificent railway system—greater, in proportion to population, than any other country in the world; and will almost immediately commence the construction of a Great Trunk Railway, to connect the mouth of the St. Lawrence with the harbour of Victoria in British Columbia. It constitutes, it has been justly said, "no Elysium of pleasure, no Utopia of wealth, but a country in which an industrious emigrant may form for himself a happy home, and enjoy the greatest of human blessings—independence and health; and to these advantages are added political freedom for himself, free education for his children, a pure administration of justice, and a fair prospect of affluence as the reward of industry and economy." The appropriate motto of the capital is, "Industry, Intelligence, and Integrity;" and her emblem is the beaver.

The neighbouring states of Nova Scotia, New Brunswick, and Prince Edward's Island, which together possess a total population of 650,000, are not equally prosperous; but much may be hoped from their confederation with Canada under the general title of the "Dominion of Canada."

II.—RUPERT'S LAND AND THE RED RIVER TERRITORY.

Canada, and the confederated provinces of New Brunswick, Nova Scotia, and Prince Edward's Island, although at present the most important portion of British North America, form but a comparatively small slice of that extensive region which, stretching from the Atlantic to the Pacific, and touching the United States at the great lakes in the 49th parallel, is limited to the north only by the Frozen Ocean. A large but rather indefinite section of the British territory north of Canada is known as Rupert's Land, and was formerly the hunting-ground of the Hudson's Bay Company. "Imagine," says Mr. R. M. Ballantyne, "an immense extent of country, many hundred miles broad, and many hundred miles long, covered with dense forests, expanded lakes, broad rivers, and mighty mountains, and all in a state of primeval simplicity, undefaced by the axe of the civilized man, and untenanted, save by a few roving hordes of Red Indians, and myriads of wild animals. Picture amid this wilderness a number of small squares, each enclosing about half-a-dozen wooden houses, and about a dozen men, and between each of these establishments a space of forest, varying from fifty to three hundred miles in length, and you will have a pretty correct idea of the Hudson's Bay territories. The idea, however, may be still more correctly obtained by imagining populous Great Britain converted into a wilderness, and planted in the middle of Rupert's Land. The Company, in that case, would build three forts in it—one at Land's End, one in Wales, and one in the Highlands; so that in Britain there would be but three hamlets, with a population of some thirty men, half-a-dozen women, and a few children. The Company's posts extend, with these intervals, from the Atlantic to the Pacific Ocean, and from within the Arctic Circle to the northern boundaries of the United States." Exclusive of flying posts, the Company had in all one hundred and sixty-four regular establishments. Some idea of the extensive character of its operations may be derived from the fact that about thirty thousand buffaloes were annually slain on its ground, to say nothing of elks, martens, and other animals. The proprietary system under which the Company held this vast territory, by a charter of Charles II., confirmed by subsequent Acts of Parliament, was naturally repugnant to modern views. So great a monopoly, and such uncontrolled power, cannot be exercised by any body of private traders without grave abuses. The Hudson's Bay Company was accused, even by some of its own servants, of very cruel and despotic behaviour. It was said that the Indians were cheated when disposing of their furs; that exorbitant prices were exacted from them for the arms and ammunition without which they could not earn their living; and that they were systematically reduced to a state of helpless and miserable dependence on the officials of the Company.

It was added that an expert trapper might take the life of an Indian with impunity; and that the subordinate officials were in the habit of shooting or hanging natives, after a mockery of a trial, on the mere suspicion of wrong-doing. Many of these stories, of course, related to a remote period, and were probably exaggerated. But it was undeniable that the Company persisted in supplying rum in unlimited quantities to the Indians, although no spirits are allowed to be sold to them in the States; that it exerted itself to the utmost of its power to enshroud its territories in a veil of mystery; and that, instead of promoting, it obstructed exploration. It endeavoured to convey an idea that its domain was a desolate and inhospitable land, in which only rude, hardy trappers could endure to reside, and that it was fitted for nothing save a great game preserve. It is perfectly true that a large portion of the territory is a desert, in which winter reigns with Arctic severity; but it also comprises large tracts of valuable timber, prairies capable of supporting numerous flocks and herds, and soil adapted for cultivation.

Except recently at Vancouver's Island, the Red River was the only point at which the Company permitted colonization to be carried on. In 1811, the Earl of Selkirk transported thither a body of Highlanders; not so much, it is suspected, with the view of peopling the country as of placing an obstacle in the way of a rival company of fur-traders. In spite of the early troubles with which it had to contend, in repeated visitations of grasshoppers, inundations from the swollen river, the difficulty of procuring stock and implements, and the want of a market, the little settlement has taken firm root. It now comprises a thriving British community of whites and half-breeds, numbering about six thousand five hundred souls, and separated from the nearest point of civilization by four hundred miles of wilderness. For forty miles along the river there is a straggling chain of small farming establishments, interspersed with churches and windmills. The soil is very rich, and yields heavy crops of grain. Bleating flocks and lowing herds cover the pastures. A happy future may be expected for the whole territory now that it is associated with other provinces in the Dominion of Canada.

III.—VANCOUVER'S ISLAND AND BRITISH COLUMBIA.

Although formerly two distinct colonies, Vancouver's Island and British Columbia were often spoken of as an united settlement, and the expectation has, of late years, been fulfilled. Vancouver's Island is the elder. Established in 1849, under the auspices of the Hudson's Bay Company, in fulfilment of a condition attached by the Government to the renewal of their charter, the colony had at first but a feeble existence, and but for the magnetic attraction of the gold-fields on the other side of the Georgia Channel, it would have remained in the same undeveloped state, if it had not died out altogether. Viewed from seaward, the island presents rather an unprepossessing appearance. Dark frowning cliffs girdle its shores; beyond these, with scarcely any interval of level land, rounded hills, densely covered with fir, rise one above the other; and over these, again, appear bare, rugged mountains, with peaks jagged like the edge of a saw. The whole centre of the island, as far as it has been explored, is said to be a mass of rock and mountain. Although there is not much open land, it is exceedingly fertile. Victoria, the capital, is situated on undulating ground overlooking the bay. Four years ago it was a mere trading port of the Hudson's Bay Company, and contained about 250 people. Its population has now risen to between 6000 and 7000. Broad streets of substantial wooden houses have been erected. A few brick stores, a handsome stone bank, the spires of four churches, one or two Government buildings, and the high, spiked walls of a jail, distinguish the place from a mere log-town, and indicate its pretensions to be regarded as a capital.* Suburbs, shaded with oak trees like an English park, and rich agricultural land, surround the town. Although there is a harbour at

---

* In Victoria there are gas-works, an iron foundry, machine shops, a public library and reading-room, two newspapers, two fire companies, a St. Andrew's Society, a Freemasons' Lodge, a Horticultural Society, a Philharmonic Society, a gymnasium, bowling-alley, a jockey club, theatre, &c.

Victoria, it is not so good as that at Esquimoult, which is beginning to rise into notice. Half a dozen houses, three or four grog shops, and one or two stores, represent at present the "town" of Esquimoult. Vancouver's Island is rich in coal, which is of great value in that part of the world, California being deficient in that important mineral. The population of Vancouver's Island (which is equal in size to the half of Ireland) is estimated as follows:— 6700 whites (of whom 700 are women), 500 coloured people, and 15,000 Indians.

Sailing through the Strait of St. Juan de Fuca, on his right the traveller beholds the snow-capped mountains of Washington territory; to the left lies Vancouver's Island, low in comparison with the opposite shore, but still possessing heights on which, even in June, patches of snow glisten. The glassy waters of the Gulf of Georgia present a striking appearance, dotted with many little islands, and enlivened by swiftly-gliding canoes, filled with painted Indians, slow-paced sailing ships, and spluttering steamers. On the side of the gulf, opposite to Vancouver's Island, loom the dark shores of British Columbia. At first sight, the whole country appears to be clothed with forest; but when the traveller moves inland, he learns that, in the lowlands, the pines frequently take the form of belts, enclosing rich valleys and open prairies; lawns, in which oaks and maples, not pines, predominate; marshes, covered with long, coarse grass; and lakes, fringed with flowering shrubs, willows, and poplars.* "The impressions which this country leaves on the mind," says Mr. Macdonald, C.E., "are of grandeur, gloomy vastness, awful solitude, rendered more dismal by the howl of beasts of prey. Streams, white with foam, flow amid cliffs and ravines, forming at places magnificent waterfalls, whose lonely thunder swells and dies away in the interminable solitude of unpeopled space. Tremendous precipices, yawning gulfs, and towering rocks, whose naked backs have withstood the storms of six thousand years, are all there to astonish and rivet the attention. Forests of the deepest green present to the eye vast masses of foliage, fresh and glittering in the sunlight; whilst, far above, overhanging cliffs and mountains, gleam piles and pyramids of snow, and ice, and glacier gorges, of remarkable splendour. The surface of the country is generally rocky, except where covered with forest trees and underwood." The deer, the elk, the bear, the puma, and the wolf, people the fastnesses of the forest; and there are vast well-stocked covers of grouse, partridges, and various kinds of wild-fowl. Fish swarm along the shores, and in the numerous lakes which stud the country. The salmon is especially abundant. The Indian, by a few hauls of the net, fills his canoe with them. The bear sits by the side of the river, and paws them out for breakfast,

* "Facts and Figures," by Mr Despard Pemberton.

dinner, and supper. The Hudson's Bay Company salts annually about two thousand barrels of salmon. There is a great diversity of climate, both in British Columbia and Vancouver's Island. The white fox and the humming-bird, the reindeer's lichen and the cactus, may be found within the limits of one territory. Generally speaking, the climate of the sea-coast is milder and finer than that of England, but wet in winter. In the interior the winters are drier and colder, while the summers are hotter.

New Westminster, the capital of British Columbia, stands on the bank of the Fraser River, about fifteen miles from its mouth. It has only 300 inhabitants, but it boasts a church, school, custom-house, jail, barracks, treasury, mint, and assay office. One or two Indian villages in the gold regions are beginning to be transformed into white settlements. With an area about three and a half times as large as Great Britain, British Columbia has a population of 20,000 whites (of which a comparatively small number are women), 2000 Chinamen, and from 10,000 to 15,000 Indians. The aborigines have generally shown themselves friendly; but the outrages which some of the ruffians, attracted by the gold diggings, have perpetrated, have naturally provoked reprisals.

At present British Columbia is living on its gold-fields. The chief fields are situated in the newly discovered district of Cariboo (a corruption from Cerf-bœuf, a large species of reindeer which inhabits the country), near the sources of Fraser River. This district is described as a

> "Land of brown heath and shaggy wood,
> Land of the mountain and the flood;"

for it is a rugged mass of hills and streams,—in the lower parts swampy and heavily timbered with extensive forests, and covered with a dense brushwood in the higher latitudes. The only level ground is found on the tops of the mountains, which are all flat. Ravines abound, along the sides of which run what the miners call "benches," or terraces, which resemble the well-known parallel roads of Glen Roy in Scotland. These benches, as far as they have been tested, have yielded gold. The only portion of the district that has been explored is a patch of country fifty miles from north to south, and thirty miles from east to west. It bears a striking resemblance to the richest regions of California, and exhibits all the characteristics of an auriferous country. As far as "prospecting" has yet gone, this character has been fully established. The country exhibits the marks of strong volcanic action, and veins and boulders of quartz (gold matrix) are seen in every direction in the hills. These, however, have been hitherto neglected by the most of the "diggers" for the placeres, on account of the latter being much more easily worked. "There is an efflorescence of gold," says one writer, "near the surface in the virgin soil of most gold-bearing countries; but I never knew it so general as it is in British Columbia. The gold is found a few inches, a foot or two, and very seldom more than six feet, below the surface. The gold is all coarse gold, granulated, gravelly stuff, mixed with pellets and pebbles of pure metal of considerable size." When the diggings were first commenced, the snow lay deep on the ground, and the implements of the miners were of the rudest kind. Notwithstanding these drawbacks, they took out as much as from 50 to 400 dollars a day; results which were largely increased as soon as the weather improved, and "flumes" were constructed to economize manual labour, and enable them to discard the slow and wearisome "cradle." By the end of last year, the deposits were found to be not only rich, but extensive, and "tunnelling" was resorted to in the sides of the hills. The prizes which some of the miners have made appear marvellous. For instance, in two months five men obtained £20,000 worth of gold. The total yield of gold over the whole country for 1861 gave 6,791,409 dollars, as the earnings of 5000 miners. Allowance must be made, however, for the necessarily high prices of provisions. A meal of beans and bacon with a cup of wretched coffee cost 8s. 4d.; and 2s. per square inch was charged for water for sluicing. At the diggings the cost of living was about £12, 10s. a day. Mr. Macdonald therefore calculates that, regarded as a whole, the mining was a losing game, since the expenditure for food, apparatus, &c., in 1861, exceeded the return of gold by 42,614,836 dollars. If fortunes were gained, fortunes must also have been lost at Cariboo.

Another gold region has lately been discovered to the north of the northern limits of British Columbia, in the Indian land, known as the Stickeen country. This district is of vast extent, and belongs to Great Britain, with the exception of a strip or belt on the Pacific, which was ceded to Russia in 1825. Several hundred miners are now at work along the banks of the Stickeen River.

The chief value of British Columbia lies in the fact that it will ere long be traversed by a great highway leading from the Atlantic to the Pacific. We may look forward, moreover, to its speedy annexation to the Canadian Dominion, which cannot fail to stimulate its prosperity.

The Australian Continent.

I.—BOTANY BAY.
II.—THE AUSTRALIAN PASTURES.
III.—THE GOLD DIGGINGS.
IV.—THE AUSTRALIAN INTERIOR.

The Australian Continent.

I.—BOTANY BAY.

THE term, "our Antipodes," as applied to Australia, is justified not merely by its position on the globe, but by the many contrasts which it offers to the mother country. "It is in New Holland," says one shrewd observer, "where it is summer when it is winter in Europe, and *vice versa;* where the barometer rises before bad weather, and falls before good; where the north is the hot wind, and the south the cold; where the humblest house is fitted up with cedar; where the fields are fenced with mahogany, and myrtle-trees are burned for fuel; where the swans are black and the eagles are white; where the kangaroo, an animal between the squirrel and the deer, has five claws on its fore paws and three talons on its hind legs, like a bird, and yet hops on its tail; where the mole lays eggs and has a duck's bill; where there is a bird with a broom in its mouth instead of a tongue; where the pears are made of wood, with the stalk at the broader end; and where the cherry grows with the stone on the outside." "Truly a strange land," adds another writer, "where pigs are fattened on peaches, and hundreds of thousands of fat sheep and oxen are annually boiled down for the sake of their tallow, to the waste of untold quantities of excellent beef and mutton." It is a proof of the robust vitality of our national character, that, notwithstanding these and many other differences between England and Australia, our great colony should bear so truly English a character. English plants and animals are affectionately cherished, English manners and customs are retained, and the appearance of English towns is carefully imitated.

By which nation Australia was discovered is a matter of doubt. The preponderance of land on the north side of the globe, as portrayed in the maps of the sixteenth century, suggested to many minds the existence of a great continent in the south; and Spanish and Portuguese navigators, adopting this theory, reported the discovery of a "great south land," which some of them connected with Java, and others with America. Whether any of them really came upon a part of Australia, or whether they mistook detached islands for portions of the mainland, there is no direct testimony to show. A chart has lately been discovered, in the British Museum, which is said to prove that the first discovery of Australia was made in 1601, by Manuel di Eredia. In the narrative of Captain Flinders mention is made of charts in the same repository dating as far back as 1542, in which the north and north-west coasts of Australia are pretty accurately laid down under the name of Great Java. It is at least certain that the Dutch visited Australia in the seventeenth century. Between 1606 and 1636, various searching expeditions sailed from Holland, and succeeded, although without always knowing it, in touching various points on the continental coast. The results of these voyages were at the time reckoned of little worth: all that was found was, according to one chronicler, "everywhere shallow water and barren coasts, and islands thinly peopled by divers cruel, poor, and brutal nations." Tasman was more successful. In 1642 he circumnavigated the whole of Australia, but without visiting any part of it, during the voyage in which he discovered Van Diemen's Land and New Zealand. Two years later he is supposed to have sailed round the Gulf of Carpentaria. The subsequent expeditions of the Dutch added but little to our knowledge of Australia, which to all practical intents and purposes remained unexplored till the English turned their attention to the matter. Dampier twice visited it,—the first time when on his celebrated buccaneering voyage round the world, and afterwards when more legitimately engaged as the commander of a royal exploring expedition. He found shoals of sharks along the coast, and on shore a number of the "most unpleasant-looking and worst featured of any people" he had ever seen. Nearly seventy years after Dampier, Captain Cook passed that way in the *Endeavour*, and explored the whole east coast of Australia, from Cape Howe to Cape York. Striking the continent in the south, and proceeding northwards, he entered an inlet on which he conferred the name of Botany Bay, from the great variety of new plants which were there discovered. A few inhabitants were espied, but these were so shy and suspicious, that they could not be induced to approach the strangers. Resuming his voyage, Cook found the country growing more hilly, and the navigation of the coast more dangerous and intricate. One night the ship struck on a coral reef and was well-nigh lost. Fortunately, however, the rock had itself repaired the leak which it had caused, by leaving a large piece of coral to stop up the aperture in the timbers of the ship! Accordingly, when the vessel again floated, the leakage did not increase. The navigators took shelter in an adjoining cove, where they encamped for a short time. Here the natives appeared somewhat more familiar, but afforded them no assistance. Indeed the poor creatures were, perhaps, more in want of food than the crew; and when refused a share of the turtle which the sailors had procured, in revenge, fired the long grass which grew round the tents. When the ship was again fit for sea, Cook resumed the perilous navigation of the coral-reefs, and discovered the channel which separates Australia from New Guinea. Landing on a little island, to which he gave the appropriate name of Possession, he took possession, in the name of King George, of the immense line of coast which he had surveyed. In this expedition Cook "reaped the harvest of discovery; but the gleanings of the field remained to be gathered." Bass, Flinders, and Grant proved themselves fully capable of continuing the work which Cook had inaugurated, and within fifty years after the English entered on the work of exploration, they had surveyed the outline of the continent, with the exception of a small gap between Flinders' and Grant's Lands.

The first use of this noble continent was as a jail. The exile and enslavement of prisoners are practices of ancient date. When colonization began, the transportation of convicts to a distant settlement satisfied at once the desire of the government to relieve the mother country from troublesome subjects, and to turn their services to profitable account. Almost from the first establishment of the English colonies, large numbers of prisoners were handed over to court favourites, who sold them into bondage in the "plantations." This ingenious method of punishing the unruly and disaffected, and at the same time rewarding the adherents of the government, was highly approved by King James II. Monmouth's rash rebellion afforded a pretext for the banishment in this way of a great many unfortunate persons. After the rupture with the American colonies in 1776, and the failure of the penal settlements on the west coast of Africa, the English government was at a loss how to dispose of the criminal population. The prisons were frightfully overcrowded, and it was necessary that some new convict stations should be found. In its perplexity, the government recollected the favourable accounts given of the two thousand miles of coast at the other end of the world, upon which Captain Cook had bestowed the name of New South Wales, and of which he had taken possession in the name of his sovereign. It was determined to despatch a body of convicts, to lay the foundation of a colony in that country.

In 1787, a fleet of eleven sail conveyed to Botany Bay 600 male and 250 female convicts, with a guard of marines. No sooner had they arrived, than Captain Phillip, who commanded the expedition, at once pronounced the place unsuitable, the anchorage being unsafe, and the land sterile and inhospitable. Cruising about in search of a better situation, he found, a few miles further north, a narrow opening in the precipitous, iron-bound coast. Passing up this inlet, he unexpectedly entered a vast land-locked lake, which at a glance was seen to be one of the finest harbours in the world. The day was calm and bright, and as the strangers sailed along, they observed with delight the magnificent groves which crowned the shores, and the beautiful islets dotting the expanse of waters. The fleet was immediately brought round to this inviting spot. On the 26th January 1788, the British flag was hoisted at Sydney Cove, a small inlet on the south side of the Bay, where the troops and convicts disembarked. The entire company numbered 1030. Distress and privation beset them almost from their first landing. In despatching the expedition, there had been no attempt at selection or organization. There were not half a dozen men among them who knew how to use a carpenter's tools, and there was only one bricklayer. Not a mechanic could be found capable of erecting an ordinary corn-mill. The building of houses, therefore, proceeded slowly. The officers and marines enjoyed the luxury of tents; but many of the convicts had to be thankful for the shelter of a cave among the rocks, or the hollow of an old tree. Promising as the shores of the bay looked on the sunny day when the English first beheld them, they soon learned that the soil was sandy and barren, and that every yard required for cultivation must be won from the forest, by cutting down trees so hard that they turned the edges of the best axes, and almost baffled the efforts of the most skilled wood-cutters. No game was to be found, except an occasional emu or stray kangaroo. It was impossible, therefore, that they could support themselves. The rations which they brought with them were soon consumed. Confined on a narrow strip of desert shore, with the grim and rugged heights of the Blue Mountains on one side, and the boundless ocean on the other, famine appeared inevitable. Before they had been a year at Sydney, there were not four months' provisions in the settlement, even at half-allowance. The government store-ship was wrecked on its way out to the colony; but, fortunately, its cargo was saved, and forwarded to the relief of our starving countrymen.

Without waiting to learn how the settlement had thriven, the government despatched thither ship after ship, laden with prisoners of all degrees of crime. The simple country lad, who had snared a hare or knocked over a pheasant, and had had, perhaps, a scuffle with the squire's keepers, was coupled with the hardened ruffian who had spent a life of crime. Corrupted by such companionship, and goaded by want and tyranny, the least guilty, before long, became as bad as the worst. Sometimes half of a ship load of the poor wretches would perish on the voyage, and those who survived would scarcely be able to crawl upon deck and jump into the boats when the vessel came to anchor in Sydney Cove. Once on shore, their misery did not cease, but assumed merely a new, and perhaps a more aggravated form. There was no limit to the despotism of the military officers. The governor had absolute power in the settlement, —could set a convict at liberty, cut his back into raw flesh with the lash, or hang him up to the nearest tree at a moment's notice. The officers were also tyrants in their degree. No regular overseers were sent out from England. The biggest and strongest convicts were selected for the task, and they were generally the most brutal. A prisoner who was useful to the officers could do almost anything with impunity; but any one who did not possess that qualification was, for the most trifling offence, flogged or hanged without mercy. The women were not dealt with more leniently than the men. "The women who misbehaved," says one of those who early arrived in the colony, "were put in iron-spiked collars. Six hundred died out of eight hundred at Toongabbie." Years passed before there was a church in the colony. As the convicts were assembled for service under a broiling sun or pelting rain, it was no wonder that they regarded it as a penance rather than a rite. Food was always scarce. "I have often," said one of the convicts, "taken grass and pounded it, and made soup from the native dog. I would eat anything then. Any man would have committed a murder, ay, three murders, for a month's provisions." "For a long period," said another, "my ration was only a cob or single head of corn in a day, and for three years I lived under a constant apprehension that I should perish of hunger." It was a long time before sufficient grain was grown to feed the settlement; and for fifteen years fresh meat was a rare luxury to the authorities, while meat was almost unknown to the convicts. The settlement was, in fact, as has been truly said, a population of slaves and slave-drivers, who did not colonize, but were encamped upon the land they occupied.

II.—THE AUSTRALIAN PASTURES.

The process, as one of the governors who succeeded Captain Phillip phrased it, of turning pickpockets into ploughmen was attended with but scant success, and free settlers arrived in very slender numbers. The voyage was an expensive one, and there was, indeed, nothing tempting in the life of the colony. In 1792 there were sixty-seven settlers, holding under grant 3470 acres, of which only 417 acres were under cultivation. There was some talk of abandoning this costly and unproductive experiment, when an incident occurred which had an important effect on the future destiny of the colony. A band of natives came to the neighbourhood of Sydney to celebrate one of their festivals. The settlers observed that in some of their dances they imitated the bellowing and butting of cattle. No native cattle had hitherto been seen. The "black fellows" were questioned as to the meaning of the sounds and signs which they made. They replied that on their way to Sydney they had seen a great herd of wild cattle feeding, near large pools in an open forest. Scouts were immediately sent out, who confirmed their report. The event was deemed of such importance, that the governor himself and his staff paid a visit to the herd; which proved to be of the Cape breed, humphy on the shoulders and with long horns. During the first year of the colony, four cows and a couple of bulls strayed into the woods, in search, probably, of a better supply of fodder. As they never returned, it was supposed that they had perished in the wilds; but there can be no doubt that the herd which was now discovered was the offspring of the wanderers. Mr. John M'Arthur, an officer in the colonial garrison, endowed with great foresight, and of an enterprising spirit, was struck by the good sense and discrimination of the cattle, in exchanging their miserable quarters by the sea-shore for such a capital grazing-ground as that in which they were found. So he settled in the same district, and devoted himself to stock-breeding. In this pursuit he was successful beyond expectation, and his example was followed by many. But M'Arthur not only led the way in the rearing of cattle; he introduced a superior breed of sheep. His keen, observing eyes, did not fail to mark the improvement which took place in the coats of the hairy Bengal and fat-tailed Cape sheep, after a brief residence in the colony; and then it struck him that there were many points of resemblance in soil and climate between Spain and Australia. Acting on this idea, he imported a number of the famous

Spanish merinoes, which took to their new country in the most kindly manner; and Australia is now the greatest wool-growing country in the world.*

Attracted by the success of this new enterprise, free settlers began gradually to arrive in greater numbers, though for a long time they were far exceeded by the convict class. Sydney was now a thriving little town. Except the governor's mansion, which was of stone, and one or two brick houses occupied by officials, most of the dwellings consisted of only plastered logs and shingled roofs; but as they were snug and comfortable, the inhabitants were content. Their harbour was the finest in the world, sending its arms in among their cottages and gardens. Every year, in the season, a number of whalers sailed out of it for a cruise in the great Southern Ocean, and returned laden with black oil and sperm. A trade in various other commodities was also springing up; and the colonists were sadly hampered for want of space. They required more extensive pasture-grounds for their sheep than lay between the waters of the Bay and the Blue Mountains; but those rugged heights seemed insurmountable. The natives declared that they were haunted by a race of malignant spirits, who vindictively destroyed all who dared to invade their domains. High rewards were offered for the dis-

---

* In 1860 the export of wool from Sydney was between twelve and thirteen million pounds in weight, and £1,123,609 in value. There are over six millions of sheep in the colony.

covery of any opening in the hills, of even a mere sheep track; and many brave fellows explored them zealously, clambering up and down their precipitous crags, and peeping into their black, yawning chasms. Some went forth on this mission who never were seen or heard of afterwards. Some were brought home shattered by a fall from some dizzy eminence. It was not till 1813 that Mr. Evans, a government surveyor, discovered the long sought pass; and immediately the pent-up flocks and herds of the colonists poured through it to the "fresh fields and pastures new" on the other side.

To appreciate the value of this discovery we must dissociate from the idea of grass in Australia the soft, close, velvety texture of English grass. The grass of Australia never forms turf; it grows in tufts, so that however green a plain looks in the distance, the dark soil can always be seen between the blades when you are close to it. It takes from three to five acres to feed a single sheep; and consequently the sheep-walks and cattle-runs of the great breeders range over immense tracts of country. The pass through the mountains gave access to boundless plains; but, unfortunately, the supply of water was scanty and capricious. As the flocks increase, the owners must penetrate further into the interior in search of fresh runs. The "bush" now becomes the scene of an important phase of Australian life, while the shepherd and stockman take rank as the representative men of the colony. The pastoral life is lonely and monotonous. At day-break the shepherd unpens his flock. Advancing slowly for four or five miles, they crop the grass. After an interval of repose at the hot noon-tide, the sheep are driven home again. The fare of the shepherd is perpetually the same; but it is ample. It is an unvarying course of "damper,"* grilled mutton, and tea boiled with sugar in a tin pannikin, which he always carries with him. In a country like Australia, where the number of a flock ranges from 20,000 to 50,000, the shepherd's career is not devoid of cares and dangers. The dingoe, or wild dog of the bush, may worry his sheep. He himself may be attacked by treacherous natives or ruffianly bush-rangers.

The stockman has a more exciting career than the shepherd, and is exposed to greater perils and privations. Mounted on a rough, sturdy horse, with his hat of cabbage-tree palm strapped tightly under his chin, to keep it from blowing off when he is at full gallop, with feet sheathed in slipper-stirrups of brass, and flourishing his stock whip, he presents a striking appearance. The stock whip is a very formidable weapon. To a handle of a foot and a half in length is attached a thick tapering thong, from twelve to sixteen feet long, and weighing about a couple of pounds, which is finished off with a

---

* Flour and water kneaded together and baked in flat cakes amongst the ashes of a wood fire.

"cracker." The stockman prides himself upon his skill in wielding this instrument. At a considerable distance he can flick a fly off the ear of an ox, or cut a piece out of the animal's back, if he deem such correction necessary. When he cracks the whip the noise is like a discharge of musketry, and is of itself quite sufficient to recall any well-regulated beast to a sense of its P's and Q's. He must be a resolute, ready-witted fellow, for his charge are often as shy as they are refractory. Sometimes a whole herd will go off silently through the night in Indian file, and the stockman has to gallop back for miles, and perhaps for days, before he recovers the deserters. He has to follow the cattle across hills and plains, through forests and rivers, sometimes on horseback, sometimes wading or swimming. He may have to gallop at full speed at noon, when the thermometer is at 140 degrees; and to sleep on the ground, with only a rug for a covering, amid a pelting rain, with the thermometer at 40°. There is a story of one who passed the whole night in a deluge of rain, sitting on a saddle to keep him off the flooded ground, and holding another saddle over his head as a substitute for an umbrella! Traversing a wider tract of country than the shepherd, the stockman is more exposed to attack from bush-rangers or hostile natives. There are, however, two grave dangers which both share in common. One is a fire in the bush. This terrible catastrophe has been often described, but perhaps never so graphically as by Mr. W. Howitt in the following extract. It relates to the great conflagration of "Black Thursday," which desolated so wide a tract of country, on the 6th February 1851:—

"What a scene! The woods were flaming and crackling in one illimitable conflagration. The wind dashing from the north in gusts of inconceivable heat, seemed to tear the very face and shrivel up the lungs. The fire leaped from tree to tree, flashing and roaring along with the speed and destructiveness of lightning. The sear foliage seemed to match the fire, and to perish in it in a riot of demoniacal revelry. On it flew, fast as the fleetest horse could gallop; and consuming acres of leaves in a moment, still remained to rage and roar amongst the branches and in the hollow stems of ancient trees. There was a sound as of thunder, mingled with the crash of falling trees, and the wild cries of legions of birds of all kinds which fell scorched and blackened and dead to the ground. Now the flames came racing along the grass with the speed of the wind, and mowing all smooth as a pavement; now they tore furiously through some near point in the forest, and flung burning ashes and tangles of blazing bark upon the galloping rider. When the wind veered, the reek driven backward revealed a most amazing scene: The blazing skirts of the forest; huge isolated trees, glaring red—standing columns of fire: here, a vast troop of wild horses, with flying manes and tails, rushing with thundering hoofs over the plain; there, herds of cattle with bloodshot eyes and hanging tongues, running they knew not whither, from the fire; troops of kangaroos leaping franticly across the riders' path, their hair singed, and giving out strongly the stench of fire; birds of all kinds and colours shrieking piteously as they drove wildly by, and yet seeing no spot of safety; thousands of sheep standing huddled in terror on the scorched flats, with singed wool, deserted by their shepherds, who had fled for their lives."

The other peril which menaces both shepherd and stockman arises from the singular character of the Australian water-courses. There is a number of permanent rivers, and the country through which they run is of course quickly occupied, and jealously retained. But there are other streams, of a mysterious and delusive character. By the side of one of these a flockmaster may lead his sheep, rejoicing in the abundance of water. In one season the waters will suddenly swell into an inundation, sweeping away a tithe of his flock, and perhaps huts and homestead also. Another time a series of pools will alone mark the course of the river. Again, the water will entirely disappear, and leave the stony bed dry and dusty, while the poor sheep gasp in an agony of thirst, and strew the banks with their carcasses.

The pass through the Blue Mountains gave the

settlers abundance of land. The next object of search was water, and the colonization of the continent may be said to have kept pace with the discovery of sources of that indispensable element. Between 1813 and 1820 the courses of the Macquarie, Lachlan, and Murrumbidgee rivers were tracked. Within the next ten years, Captain Sturt discovered the river Darling, and followed the Murray from its junction with the Murrumbidgee to the sea. The new district soon swarmed with the overflowing flocks and herds of New South Wales. In a few years it was formed into a separate colony, under the name of South Australia, and Adelaide was founded.

A new class, the "overlanders," now appeared. " The overlanders," says Sir George Grey, "are nearly all men in the prime of youth, whose occupation it is to convey large herds of stock from market to market, and from colony to colony. The overlanders are generally descended from good families, have received a liberal education (Etonians and Oxonians are to be found amongst them), and even at their first start in the colonies, were possessed of what is considered an independence. Among them is to be found a degree of polish and frankness rarely to be looked for in such a mode of life; and in the distant desert you unexpectedly stumble on the finished gentleman. The magnitude of the operations of the overlanders would scarcely be credited. A whole fortune is risked, and in the wilderness." These dashing fellows wear a picturesque garb—gay flannel shirts, tall jack boots, broad brimmed *sombreros*, and belts bearing knives and pistols—and ride the best blood horses they can get.

The settlement of Victoria sprang from the pressure of overflowing flocks and herds in two opposite quarters,—New South Wales on the north, and Tasmania (Van Dieman's Land) on the south. In 1836 Major (afterwards Sir Thomas) Mitchell, pushing down the Darling and Murray, struck into a land which, from its exuberant fertility, he called Australia Felix. Settlers hastened thither from New South Wales, but found the district already inhabited by Englishmen. For years before, the whalers had carried to Tasmania glowing reports of the rich and beautiful land on the other side of Bass's Strait. Every now and again two or three convicts would conspire to escape, seize a boat, and make for the other side of the channel. Occasional settlers followed their example, as space became confined in the island. After Major Mitchell's survey in 1836, however, the Tasmanians flocked to the new settlement, meeting there a similar stream of emigration from the north. Thus the colony of Victoria was speedily peopled; and in 1837 the foundations of Melbourne were laid.

III.—THE GOLD DIGGINGS.

In the beginning of May 1851 an exciting rumour pervaded Sydney. It was said that a gold field had been discovered within the colony. Many were incredulous. How was it, they asked, that no trace of it had ever been discovered before? Others, however, recalled cases in which persons in the colony had unaccountably become possessed of gold. There was one old shepherd who used to come up to town at intervals to dispose of small quantities of the precious metal. He was watched, but no one ever discovered whence he got it; and it was supposed that he was in league with some bush-rangers, who melted down their booty. A convict also had been flogged for having a lump of gold, as no one doubted that it had been gained by robbery, and as he stubbornly refused to tell how he came by it. While people in Sydney were debating the authenticity of the news, there arrived a confirmation of it in the shape of a quantity of nuggets. Mr. E. H. Hargreaves was the discoverer. Tempted away from his farm near Bathurst to seek for gold in the Californian placers, he was persuaded, from the similarity of the geological formation, that there must be gold also near his own home. On his return he at once commenced a vigorous search, and at the end of one or two months found some gold.

No sooner was the truth established, than there

was an universal rush to the diggings. Not a pair of stout arms in the settlement would consent to do ordinary drudgery when such a golden fortune was within their reach. The business of the colony was brought almost to a stand still. The banker was deserted by his clerks; the merchant found himself alone in his warehouse. No sooner did a ship arrive in the harbour, than the crew at once ran away to the diggings. The shepherd left his sheep to take care of themselves; and the cattle wandered undisturbed by the crack of the stockman's whip, for he, too, was on the road to *El Dorado.* All the social relations of the community were at once overthrown. The governor of a province had to light his own fire and black his own boots; the sons of the chief-justice had to groom their father's horses and cook the dinner; merchants had to deliver their own goods, and store-keepers to officiate as their own porters. Ladies had to do kitchen work, and the large flock-masters had to employ even their little children to tend the sheep. Not a few employers were ruined by this sudden revolution. We are told of one or two who followed their men in the vain hope of persuading them to return, and who were offered service by their former servants. Along all the roads to the gold fields poured a continuous stream of gold-seekers,—men on foot with bundles slung on the end of spades or guns; brown-bearded stockmen in red shirts, dashing along on horseback; families in white-tilted carts; huge drays loaded with stores floundering in the deep pools of mud which dotted the highway. Men of all nations were there, including Chinamen with large straw hats and wide blue trousers, shuffling along with heavy burdens swinging at the end of the long poles which they carried on their shoulders. When at night-fall the host halted, the woods resounded with the crash of falling trees, white tents glittered among the green foliage, and countless fires shed a red glare around. The inhabitants of remote, secluded homesteads, were startled by the invasion of this strange, innumerable horde, but became reconciled to it when they discovered how the price of their sheep and poultry and flour rose. Sheep were no longer killed for the wool and tallow, but were sold as meat.

The diggings presented a strange spectacle. The lonely bush, where formerly reigned a silence unbroken save by the musical note of the bell-bird, the quaint whistle of the magpie, or the grotesque hoo-hoo, ha, ha, ha, of the laughing jackass (a species of kingfisher) now resounded with a Babel of voices and a confusion of strange sounds, amid which the creaking clatter of the "cradles" rose predominant. The grassy glades, where the emu used to stalk unmolested, and the kangaroo to lead forth her young in peace, were now honey-combed with holes from ten to forty feet deep. A range of mangled stumps alone marked the site of the forest. An array of

SCENE AT THE GOLD DIGGINGS.

rude huts of stringy bark, plastered with mud and thatched with dry leaves, and tents of canvas, blankets, or bullock hides, rose in the wilderness. A legion of wild, bearded men, in scarlet shirts and tall boots, with veils tied over their faces to keep off the swarming flies, bare arms, and clothes stained with yellow mud, burrowed in the deep holes, dabbled up to the waist in the cold water of the stream while the rest of their bodies were almost melting under the sweltering glare of the sun, rocked their cradles,* or washed the precious particles out of the mud and sand in little iron pans.

In such a mixed community, engaged in a pursuit calculated to produce rather a debasing effect on the human character, there was, of course, at the outset much lawlessness and crime. The English love of order and obedience to law, however, quickly asserted itself. The government commissioner found less difficulty than was to be expected in collecting the license fees from the diggers, and the public opinion of the camp supported the authorities in the punishment of criminals.

* The "cradle" is a sort of oblong-shaped box about eight feet long. At its head is a coarse wire grating, upon which the loose earth is emptied, and which, of course, prevents the larger stones from finding their way to the interior. It stands upon "rockers,"—whence its name. The bottom of the cradle is of rounded form, with an inclination downward of half an inch or more to the foot, and has several small cleets across from side to side. A stream of water is poured through the machine, and the rockers are meanwhile kept in motion. The water gradually clears away the earthy and gravelly matter, which finds its way out at the foot, while the gold and finer particles of sand are left behind, accumulated above the upper cleets at the bottom of the cradle. Such is the rude and primitive form of gold-washing common in Australia, and introduced thither from Californian experience.—*W. Hughes.*

It was at Summerhill Creek (since called Ophir), about a hundred and forty miles from Sydney, that gold was first discovered in Australia; but the search was afterwards conducted with success along a great part of the valley of the Macquarie. At Meroo Creek there was a stone on which, doubtless, many a desperate bush-ranger had sat and smoked his pipe, planning his next foray on peaceful settlers. In the summer of 1851 that stone was found to contain a hundredweight of gold,—the largest mass of the precious metal ever heard of. Auriferous deposits, richer than those of New South Wales, were found in September 1851, in Victoria. At first it threatened the ruin of Melbourne, for it almost depopulated it; at Geelong, only a single man, it is said, at one time remained. But it soon made the fortune of the place. Melbourne was then a quiet colonial town. The arrival of a steamer was still an event, and at times there was not a vessel of any kind discharging at the Geelong wharf. When the squatters came up with their clip of wool, the streets were thronged and bustling; but that was only once a year. There were very few stone buildings, and slab-huts and weather-board houses composed the town. There were patches of grass even in some of the main thoroughfares, and in the less frequented streets bogs were not uncommon. The discovery of gold in Victoria, however, attracted vast crowds of emigrants, and Melbourne began to assume extended proportions. Houses could not be built fast enough, and Canvas Town—a confused maze of tents and booths—sprang up on the south side of the Yarra. In 1851 the population of Melbourne was ninety-five thousand. In the following year it was more than doubled, and it now holds a permanent population of over one hundred and thirty thousand. Its docks are a forest of masts. Its warehouses are of vast size and handsome appearance. A million has been spent on its broad gas-lit streets, and another million on its supply of water. This is rapid progress for a city little more than twenty years old. At the same time settled towns have sprung up at the diggings. At Ballarat, Castlemaine, Sandhurst, and other places, where a few years ago the desolate bush was tenanted only by wild beasts,—where but yesterday, as it seems, was to be seen the rude confusion of the gold-seekers' camp,—there are now handsome streets of brick and stone, imposing public buildings, miles of gas-lit thoroughfares, a police and a municipality. In the neighbourhood of every large gold field, also, immense tracts of land have been enclosed and cultivated. The colony has made 600 miles of metalled roads, and cleared 500 more; it has nearly 900 places of worship, with more than 900 public and private schools; it has a university, a public library, a museum of arts, 10 savings banks, many hospitals and asylums; but not a single work-house, (for none is needed) throughout the length and breadth of the territory.

The Australian group of colonies now comprises New South Wales, the eldest of the family; Tasmania; South Australia; Victoria; Western Australia; and Queensland, which is the youngest, being barely twelve years old. They cover an area of nearly 2,500,000 square miles, or more than twenty times the surface of the United Kingdom. They have a population of 1,500,000. They raise a revenue of more than £7,000,000 annually, and enjoy sufficient credit to have a nucleus of debt to the amount of £10,000,000. Their imports are valued at £30,000,000 a year, and their exports (chiefly gold and wool) at £27,000,000. During the last ten years, above 800 tons of gold, in value £104,649,728, or more than an eighth of our national debt, have been exported from Victoria to England. It is said that, taking the whole of Australia, each colonist has already reclaimed and cultivated twenty acres of land. The great resources of Australia as a wool-growing country have been lately augmented by Mr. Ledger,—the M'Arthur of our generation, —who, at a large expenditure, and with great difficulty, has succeeded in introducing the llama from Peru. When the government of Peru heard of his project, they prohibited the exportation of these animals; but with indomitable perseverance, aided by local knowledge and an acquaintance with the habits of the llama, Mr. Ledger collected about eight hundred of them, drove them across the Andes, and shipped them to New South Wales. At first a number of them died, but they have now become acclimatized, and are multiplying rapidly. It is estimated that before the end of the century the clip of llama wool will exceed fifty million pounds in weight. Cotton has also been cultivated with success in Queensland, which promises to rival India in supplying the mother country with the invaluable material of one of our chief manufactures.

In any account of the colonization of Australia, however brief, mention must not be omitted of the labours of Mrs. Caroline Chisholm. We have seen how the magnetic attraction of gold peopled the colonies; but the emigrants who were thus tempted across the seas were not of the best class. A large proportion of them were men of broken fortunes and doubtful character; and women being in an insignificant minority, the elevating and refining influence of the gentler sex—one of the most valuable agents of civilization—was almost wholly wanting. Visiting Sydney with her husband, an officer in the Madras army, on furlough, Mrs. Chisholm at once detected this evil, and with noble enterprise sought to provide a remedy. She established a Home in Sydney, where young friendless women were received on their arrival in the colony, and where emigrants who desired to proceed inland, obtained information and advice. Finding that there was a great demand, not merely for domestic servants, but for wives among the stock-breeders in the bush, and that many girls were frightened to proceed alone, Mrs. Chisholm collected a party, and herself led them to their destination. Such success attended the journey, that similar expeditions were organized. Every year her journeys became longer, and her parties larger. She went from farm to farm, and anxiously scrutinized the character of any family among whom she consented to leave one of "her children," as she called her charges. The settlers fully appreciated her exertions, and supplied her liberally with lodgings, provisions, horses, and drays. Shepherds would leave their work, and walk thirty or forty miles to the station where she camped, in order to choose a wife, bringing with them certificates of character and their saving-bank books. To be one of Mrs. Chisholm's young women was deemed a strong recommendation. By the end of 1842 she had succeeded in placing comfortably two thousand emigrants of both sexes. Next she visited England, and established a system of emigration in which domestic ties were respected, and by which family groups were transplanted to the other side of the globe. Her true womanly instinct taught her that the family principle is the true basis of all sound and permanent civilization. With less than £2000, between 1850 and 1855, she sent out to Australia more than a thousand colonists, and all of a superior class.

IV.—THE AUSTRALIAN INTERIOR.

Singular as it may sound to many, the only large tract of the earth's surface of which we were, until very lately, utterly ignorant, consisted of British territory. No doubt there was, as there is still, an immense area of African soil on which no European ever set eye or foot. No doubt there are wide districts in South America with which even the rulers of the land have no acquaintance. No doubt Mongolia is barely known even to the Chinese; while the grim Jotuns of frost and snow have suffered the invasion of but a small part of their polar realms. But then in every one of these cases we had learned enough of the land in question to define its general character with tolerable accuracy. The interior of Australia, however, was still an utter blank. Popular conjecture pictured it as another Sahara, as barren but more extensive than that of Africa,—a desert, which in summer was a hollow basin of burning sand, and in the rainy season a vast shallow sea. It was the dream of some romantic *savans* that the inland waste of waters might perhaps prove to be the retreat of the huge old saurians, and that the dodo and the pterodactyle might be found skimming across its breast.

Hemmed in for twenty-five years by the steep, forbidding heights of the Blue Mountains, the settlers of Port Jackson no sooner surmounted that barrier than they began to extend their surveys with spirit and success. Exploration, however, was almost entirely confined to the south-east corner of Australia, which is marked off by the River Darling, until, in 1847, Captain Sturt, the father of Australian discovery, penetrated into the interior, and almost touched the core of the continent. His journey to the first depôt, at Laidlaw's Ponds, lay for the most part along the grassy flats of the Darling, and was accomplished with ease. A hot sandy desert succeeded, across which his party toiled slowly and painfully. The birds flew gasping overhead. The iron yokes of the bullocks became so hot that they could not be placed on the animals for fear of burning them. When a breeze sprang up, it felt like the scorching blaze of a mighty furnace, which the travellers could not face. The country grew more dreary and inhospitable at every step. On reaching lat. 28, Sturt wrote: " We are now in the most gloomy desert man ever trod ; all the sand ridges are covered with tussocks of spinifex (a thick wiry grass generally found near the sea coast, and only in the most barren situations). These deserts are as silent as the grave." Further on he says: " Every animal has now forsaken this lonely and inhospitable region. If a bird appears, it is only for a moment, to rest its weary wings and then pass on. Birds of prey, parrots, pigeons, have all migrated to the north-west; whilst, on the other hand, pelicans, cormorants, and wild-fowl come in from that quarter. The first is a strong proof there is a better country to which the birds go; the other is equally conclusive of there being a desert or a sea between us and it." At Evelyn Creek, the second depôt, Sturt's further progress was impeded for six months by the excessive drought which prevailed. He and his companions made excursions in every direction, but not a drop of moisture could they find, save the scanty supply at the depôt, which was gradually failing before their eyes. "Here we are," says Sturt, "bound hand and foot, as it were, without the power of moving, captives in a large and gloomy prison." For nearly eight months no rain fell. It came at length, when they were almost in despair, and the novel sound of the rippling waters in a little gully close to their tents had a sweeter and more soothing sound than the finest melody they had ever heard. With four companions, Sturt pushed forward in a north-west direction. Crossing a darkgreen plain of samphire bushes dotted with the dry beds of small salt lagoons of sparkling white, they encountered a series of formidable ridges of a fiery red colour, rising one after another like gigantic waves, on the summits of which the sand lay like crests of snowy foam. Beyond lay an immense stony desert; which in turn gave place to a wide earthy plain, on the surface of which neither herb nor stone was visible. As they advanced the heat became more intolerable, vegetation faded out of sight, and almost every drop of water had evaporated. Drought and the indisposition of one of the party compelled a retreat. Starting again for the depôt with two men, Sturt followed a route to the east of his former track, in the hope of avoiding the grim stony desert. At Cooper's Creek he found abundance of water and rich vegetation. A tribe of some four hundred natives inhabited the spot, subsisting on the seeds of a coarse grass, which they stacked and threshed. This pleasant scene was quickly exchanged for a sterile plain, on the other side of which lay the arid, adamantine region, which the explorers were so anxious to avoid. Sturt shuddered as he beheld once more the stony waves, which stretched in an unbroken line across the horizon. Again the lack of water and the exhaustion of his men and horses prevented a further advance. With deep reluctance Sturt retraced his steps, having reached 24° 30′ lat., 137° 59′ long. in his first, and 25° 58′ lat., 139° 36′ long. in his second expedition.

Up to 1860 all subsequent attempts to explore the interior proved futile and disastrous. Eyre was twice baffled in endeavouring to penetrate from the south-east. Poor Leichardt, starting from the east, vanished into the mysterious region fifteen years ago, and has never since been heard of. Kennedy, in a similar attempt, was murdered by the natives. The elder Gregory, in 1856, tracked the Victoria River till it disappeared in a desert in lat. 18. It was not till Mr. M'Donell Stuart put forth his hand that the veil was lifted from the interior of the great Australian continent.

Mr. Stuart had already distinguished himself as a companion of Captain Sturt in 1847, and as the discoverer in 1858 of eighteen hundred square miles of valuable territory, well supplied with water, and covered with luxuriant vegetation, to the northward of Spencer's Gulf. In the latter expedition, with two attendants, and no other instruments save his watch and compass, he pushed through a marshy, saline desert, which lay between the sea and the inland country, and encountered difficulties and dangers which would have appalled any less intrepid pioneer.

Early in 1860 Mr. Stuart set out from Adelaide, again with only two companions, to go from south to north, right across the continent. On quitting Chamber's Creek, Stuart, profiting by the experience he had derived on his former visit to that quarter, took a northerly course slightly tending to the west, and, more fortunate than Sturt, succeeded in keeping clear of the stony desert. On the 23d April he reared a cone of stones, and hoisted the British flag on a mount (Central Mount Stuart) about two miles from the centre of Australia. Thus far his path had lain through a well watered, and, on the whole, fertile country. He had crossed two magnificent creeks; one of which, the Neales, at a point where several tributaries joined, spread out into a sheet of water a mile in width; while the other, the Myall, was more than one hundred and thirty yards from bank to bank. In lat. 26 he came upon another fine creek, the Frew, which fed numerous large waterholes, and was surrounded by plains of luxuriant grass, wild oats, wheat, and rye. Innumerable small creeks and pools were also met with, as well as a large reservoir of water three hundred feet in circumference, and from twelve to twenty feet deep. Towards the centre the country assumed somewhat of a tropical aspect, being dotted with India-rubber and cork trees, and a palm with small broad light-green leaves, bearing a large nut, the kernel of which resembles that of a cocoa nut, and has, when roasted, the flavour of a potato. It was in the attempt to cross from the centre to the northern coast that Mr. Stuart underwent the greatest perils and privations. "After making the centre," he writes, " I was assailed by that dreadful disease the scurvy, which completely prostrated me, and rendered me quite helpless. Still I persevered, and endeavoured to reach the mouth of the Victoria River on a north-west course, but was obliged to relinquish the attempt three separate times through want of water. The country in which I got the first course was an immense plain of red light soil, covered with nothing but spinifex and large gum trees,—not a blade of grass. On this the horses were three days, without a drop of water; and had I not been fortunate enough to drop in with a native well, I should have lost nearly all of them I then tried again twice to the eastward to round this horrid plain. The result was the same. I was now forced to go back into the centre." The retreat was not commenced a day too soon. A journey of one hundred and twelve miles under a scorching sun, and over a hot sandy soil, without water for one hundred and one hours, exhausted the explorers, and drove the horses into a frenzy through intense thirst. Three of the animals perished by the way. Stuart next made two resolute efforts to reach the Gulf of Carpentaria. His first excursion was brought to an abrupt termination by want of water. His second expedition was more fortunate, and led him northward through a beautiful and fertile district, where there were several fine water-holes, and creeks swarming with fish and water-fowl. Although the country became subsequently more sandy, and yielded no other vegetation than spinifex and dense scrub, the explorers would no doubt have traversed it had it not been for the hostile attacks of the natives. Hitherto the few aborigines whom they had met had either fled in terror or behaved peaceably, but they now mustered in large numbers, beset their track, and attempted to cut them off from the waterholes. At last the natives openly assailed them. "It was nearly dark," says Stuart, "when they came upon us, and we were in the middle of a small scrub. There was no sign whatever of any of them being near as we approached the creek. The moment we entered the scrub they were upon us. Every bush seemed to have hidden a man. Upwards of thirty attacked us in front. How many more endeavoured to surround us and cut us off from our pack-horses I cannot tell. They seemed to be in a great fury, moving their boomerangs about their heads, and howling to the top of their voices, also performing some sort of dance. Putting the horses on towards the creek, and placing ourselves between them and the natives, I told the men to get their guns ready, for I could see they were determined upon mischief. They paid no regard to all the signs of friendship I kept constantly making, but were still gradually approaching nearer. I felt very unwilling to fire upon them, and continued making signs of peace and friendship; but all to no purpose. An old man (the leader) who was in advance made signs with his boomerang for us to be off; which proved to be one of defiance, for I had no sooner turned my horse's head to see if that was what they wished, than we received a shower of boomerangs, accompanied by a fearful yell: they then commenced jumping, dancing, yelling, showing their arms in all sorts of postures, like so many fiends, and setting fire to the grass. I could see many others getting up from behind the bush; still I felt unwilling to fire upon them, and tried to make them understand that we wished to do them no harm. They now came within forty yards of us, and again made a charge, throwing their boomerangs, which came whistling and whizzing past our ears. One spear struck my horse. I then gave orders to fire, which stayed their mad career for a little. Our pack-horses, which were before us, took fright when they heard the firing and fearful yelling, and made off for the creek. Seeing the blacks running from bush to bush with the intention of cutting us off from them, while those in front were still yelling, throwing their boomerangs, and coming near to us, we gave them another reception, and sent Ben after the horses to drive them to a more favourable place, while Kekwick and I remained to cover our rear. We soon got in advance of our enemies, but they still kept following beyond the reach of our guns, the fearful yelling continuing, and fires springing in every direction; and it being now quite dark, with the country scrubby, and our enemies numerous, bold, and daring, we saw we could easily be surrounded and destroyed by such determined fellows as they had shown themselves to be. Seeing there was no chance with such fearful odds against us (ten to one), and knowing the disadvantages under which we laboured, I very unwillingly made up my mind to push on to last night's camp; which we did."—Stuart and his men thus escaped; but with such foes around them, and the water-holes being few and far between, it was deemed prudent to turn homeward. From the tactics displayed by the savages, Stuart was disposed to believe they had encountered white men before. On another occasion one of the natives made a masonic sign to Mr. Stuart, and evinced much satisfaction when the white man returned it, patting him on the back, and stroking his hair.

Returning in safety to Adelaide, Mr. Stuart was promptly re-equipped, and without delay set out a second time with an adequate force to complete the passage across the continent. From this journey he returned last September, without, however, having passed from sea to sea.

Having reached within ninety-five miles of the northern coast, an impenetrable forest barred his further progress. His most northerly point was 17 lat. and 133 long. The observations which he made in 1860 were fully confirmed by his explorations in 1861. He traversed many arid tracts, but on the whole the country was fruitful and valuable. He saw reason also to suspect the existence of a rich auriferous region. By this time Mr. Stuart has probably set out on a third journey to the interior. On this occasion, however, it is understood he will start from the north instead of the south coast.

Stuart having reached lat. 17 from the south, and Gregory lat. 18 from the north, the continent might be said, practically, to have been crossed from one shore to the other. Last year, however, one party of explorers actually passed from south to north. This feat was reserved for the ill-fated Burke and his companions. The newspapers have already told the story of this melancholy expedition. It was badly planned, and intrusted to incompetent hands. Five explorers, with ten European and three Sepoy attendants, and twenty-seven camels, to say nothing of horses and waggons, formed far too large and cumbrous a body for the work it had to do. The leader was ill chosen, for he possessed neither experience in exploration nor that resolution and foresight which are essential in such a post. The defection of the man in charge of the camels appears to have been unjustifiable, but it cannot be supposed to have affected the fate of the party. On the 16th December 1860, Burke, accompanied by Wills the surgeon, two men, King and Gray, with six camels, one horse, and three months' provisions, quitted Cooper's Creek, leaving behind them a depôt of stores in charge of a man named Brahe and the rest of their party. Six or seven weeks after they struck the River Flinders, which flows into the Gulf of Carpentaria. Here they left their camels and horse, and proceeded on foot towards the shore. It is not positively mentioned in the imperfect journals which have come to hand that they saw the sea; but as they were only twenty-five miles from it when they started on foot, and as, after travelling some distance, they crossed a salt marsh, arrived at a channel full of sea-water, and then moved "slowly down three miles to camp," there can be little doubt that they trod the beach of Carpentaria, and gazed upon the waters of the gulf. With the loss of Gray they made their way back to the depôt, after an absence of four months and five days,—and found it deserted. They rushed to the *cache* of provisions. All that it contained was a note stating that Brahe and his companions had departed seven hours before. Worn and weary with toil and privation, Burke and the two others saw no prospect of overtaking their friends. After a few days' repose, they started for the settled parts of South Australia, but broke down from sheer exhaustion. Returning to the depôt, their misery was aggravated by the discovery that in the interim Brahe had actually revisited it, disregarded the foot-prints of the camels, neglected to open the *cache*, in which they had left a memorandum, and gone away again. The rest of the story is heart-rending. The poor fellows tried vainly to prolong life on the seeds of a coarse trefoil called nardoo. First Burke, then Wills died, from sheer exhaustion, and King was left alone in the wilderness. The report of his gun attracted a number of natives, who ministered to his wants and restored him to a search party which had been sent after the missing explorers.

The meagre jottings contained in the journals of the expedition give scarcely any description of the country traversed. The fact, however, that the party crossed the continent shows at least that water did not fail them. The governor of Victoria has expressed a belief, founded on the information of the survivor, King, that the country around the Gulf of Carpentaria (which he suggests should be called Burke's Land) is admirably adapted for a settlement.

The latest explorer, Mr. Landsborough, has achieved a journey right across the continent (rather to the east of poor Burke's route) from the Gulf of Carpentaria to Melbourne. Mr. Landsborough says the shores of the gulf are so healthy, that "although living in the open air, and not having the best of food, the country agreed admirably with him, and there was no fever or ague among any of the party." The country through which he passed was, for the most part, "so well grassed, that the horses looked as if they had been stable-fed." The most elevated land on the Flinders is stated by Mr. Landsborough not to exceed 1000 feet.

Putting together the results obtained by the various explorers, we can now obtain an adequate idea of Central Australia. Originally, no doubt, as Sturt conjectured, an archipelago of islands, the sea bed has been raised in the course of ages, until it now forms a continuous continent. The idea of an inland sea has now been utterly exploded; and while there are, no doubt, many portions of the interior as desolate and hopeless as those which Sturt traversed, the stony desert and the plains of sand do not represent its general character. In fact, the central region is, after all, very like those other parts of the continent with which we are already acquainted;—a smooth undulating surface running into flats, and broken by the gentle swell of continuous ridges; wide grassy plains, alternating with tracts of dingy scrub and arid strips of sand; large creeks flowing for a certain distance like an ordinary river, and then mysteriously disappearing. M'Donell Stuart's researches, while they unquestionably prove the existence of a rich, well-watered country towards the north-west, would also seem to confirm Sturt's description of the more easterly region as consisting of barren spinifex plains, destitute of water; but then it should be remembered that both Stuart and Sturt visited it at a season when there was no rain, and when the intense heat produced active evaporation. The future explorer who shall traverse those parts at the proper period of the year will doubtless be able to report of them more favourably. Although it is only as it were since yesterday that the interior has been penetrated, yet, such is the rapidity with which things are managed in that great continent, (which, not only by its size, but by its population and resources, is justifying its claim to the title bestowed on it by the Irish emigrant, of "the fifth quarter of the world,") and such is the eager demand of the sheep-farmers for fresh fields and pastures, that we may look before long to see the contractor and the colonist making their appearance in Central Australia.

The Britain of the South.

I.—THE ISLANDS OF NEW ZEALAND.
II.—PROGRESS OF THE COLONY.

The Britain of the South.

I.—THE ISLANDS OF NEW ZEALAND.

SOME five centuries ago a body of savages in three canoes sailed to New Zealand from a land which lay to the north-east. A bitter feud raged among their people, and they forsook their native shores for the sake of peace. "My children," said the aged patriarch of their nation, when bidding them farewell, "the miseries of war now drive you from your fatherland; in your new home walk not in the ways of Tu, the god of battles. Live together in peace and love. So may you raise up a great and powerful race."* In their adopted country the immigrants found beauty to soothe their minds, and plenty to satisfy their wants. Everything was calculated to encourage a peaceful life and to wean them from violence and bloodshed. The soil yielded many fruits which were fit for food, the waters teemed with fish, and there were swarms of wild-fowl. But no snakes

---

* This is the native tradition. It is conjectured that the New Zealanders are of Malay origin.

lurked in the jungle, no beasts of prey made their
lair in the forest. The exiles could not, however,
subdue their hereditary passions. Strife soon broke
out, and, as families grew into tribes, war rarely
ceased among them. It was during a brief interval
of peace that Captain Cook, the celebrated navigator,
visited them. He was struck with their masculine
vigour and sagacity They understood the cultivation of the ground and the navigation of the seas,
and their dwellings and attire bespoke a higher
civilization than prevailed among the other islanders
of the Pacific. They despised beads and trinkets,
and prized spades and axes. The favourable report
concerning New Zealand and its inhabitants which he
carried to Europe was neutralized by the discovery
of the fact that they were perpetually at war with
each other, and that they were given to cannibalism.
In the course of years, however, the terror thus
excited died away. English vessels could not resist
the temptation of touching at those verdant shores,
and were often glad to recruit their crews with
New Zealanders, who, accustomed to cruise round the
island in their canoes, made apt sailors. As whalers
the natives were especially expert and daring. They
excelled all others in the precision with which they
hurled the harpoon, and in their readiness to brave
dangers from which others shrank appalled. There
is a story told of one of them, who, having failed
after repeated attempts to pierce a plunging whale,

sprang upon its back, sank with it into the surging waves, and, having thrust his harpoon into its side, swam back again to his boat. Although capable of great feats, the New Zealander was, however, restive under discipline, and indisposed to regular labour. One, having taken service on board of a whaler, was flogged for idleness. Returning to his family, he displayed his back scarred with the stripes, and incited them to revenge the indignity to which he had been subjected. They persuaded the captain and crew of the whaler to land, and then murdered and ate them. Te Pahi, a neighbouring chief, having exerted himself to save some of the victims, saw no harm in sitting down to the feast. The rumour spread that he had instigated the massacre. A body of whalers fell upon his village, and put himself and thirty of his people to death. There was now open war for several years between the two races. The New Zealanders were kidnapped and murdered by the white men; and in return, when a ship was wrecked upon the coast, or when a crew landed in search of water or provisions, the natives invariably assassinated the strangers. Hongo, a bold, resolute, and enlightened chief, became reconciled to the English, and visited our country. By his influence the hostility of the islanders to Europeans was removed. A desperate civil war now ensued, in the course of which immense numbers fell. The heads of the slain were cut off and dried, and became the first article of export for which New Zealand acquired a reputation. A cargo of embalmed heads was by no means an uncommon arrival from that quarter, till the trade was prohibited by governor Darling of New South Wales. A more legitimate export was found in the fine flax which the country produces.

Meanwhile, English, French, and Dutch whalers found it convenient to have regular stations in New Zealand, and returned from their expeditions in the great Southern Ocean to spend the winter there. During these periods of repose and inactivity, they mixed freely with the natives, and joined in the festivals and dances. Not a few of them were fascinated by the dark expressive eyes, long glossy hair, and buxom figures of the native girls, and took them to wife. The soft language and simple wiles of these wild beauties made a deep impression on the hearts of their foreign lovers, some of whom, out of pure love, consented to be tatooed, and to dress and live in the native fashion. The New Zealanders, shrewd and thrifty, found that it was advantageous to have a white man in their camp, because he could make better bargains for them with traders of his own complexion. The hand of the most winning of their daughters, with a rich dowry of land and the rank of a prince, was the usual temptation which they offered to the pale face to dwell among them; and to a weather-beaten sailor tired of tossing on the seas, a runaway convict from New South Wales, or a desponding settler, the temptation was irresistible. It is said that, at one time, there was no tribe of any size or dignity which did not include a European as an adopted son. One can conceive the strange feelings with which these men (Pakeha Maories) were agitated when, once or twice a year, the dull, monotonous round of savage life was broken, and old memories were revived, by a meeting with other Europeans. In some cases, no doubt, the man thus situated sank in the scale of humanity, stifling all noble aspirations, and approaching the level of the brute, with lower pleasures and lower pains. But, as a rule, he did perhaps more to raise his dark-skinned companions than those to drag him down. He taught his wife to sew and to cook, to appreciate the virtue of cleanliness and the propriety of seemly costume. To the tribe he disclosed those arts of life which are the first steps in civilization. Instead of a mere hut of reeds and mud, he showed them how to build a house, with a stout wooden framework, with a thatched roof, a chimney, and windows with shutters. Whaling boats took the place of rude bark canoes. The use of tools and fire-arms became familiar to the native. Pigs, sheep, and horses, corn and potatoes, were introduced. At the same time, with some of the virtues, the Pakeha Maories also sowed some of the vices of civilization, such as a taste for intoxicating drinks and a passion for gambling. There was but one church in Korarareka, the chief whaling station, but grog-shops and gambling-houses abounded. It was scarcely to be expected that a community composed of rough whalers and sealers of different nations, escaped convicts, keen and not too scrupulous traders, and proud, suspicious savages, could long remain in harmony. Frequent disputes arose, and too often they were only quenched in blood. Lynch law was the only rule. Every now and again a fit of virtuous indignation would seize the public. A victim would be selected, dipped in hot pitch, rolled in feathers, and so driven from the settlement. In the course of years, the natives became so expert in the art of barter, that they no longer required the services of their adopted sons. The latter were therefore deprived of their state and emoluments, and compelled to till the ground in order to procure the means of living. Many of them joined the settlement of Korarareka, which in 1839 contained a European population of a thousand.

II.—PROGRESS OF THE COLONY.

Traders and travellers carried to England glowing accounts of the advantages of New Zealand as a field for colonization,—its temperate climate, its fertility, the excellence of its natural harbours, the intelligence and skill of the natives. The English government had its hands full of colonial work at the time, and was not disposed to undertake the charge of a new plantation. It was only a fear lest it should fall into the hands of the French that induced us to add New Zealand to the number of our colonies. In 1840, two English settlements were formed there, —the one at Auckland, and the other at Wellington. Captain Hobson, the government agent, chose Auckland as the site of the capital, and provided for its security by a treaty of friendship and alliance with the natives; who, in return for our protection, recognised the British sovereignty. The settlement at Wellington was formed under the auspices of a public association. Colonel Wakefield, who conducted the first body of emigrants to the spot, purchased from the natives a tract of country as large as Ireland, for a quantity of blankets, guns, knives, &c., nominally valued at about £9000. This motley cargo also included razors and shaving tackle, Jews' harps, red nightcaps, and umbrellas. By the end of 1840, twelve hundred emigrants had been landed at Wellington. Two years later, there was a white population in New Zealand of eleven thousand. Various settlements had by this time been established. The settlers in the north were derived chiefly from Australia, and those in the south from Great Britain.

Although the natives at first gave the settlers a kindly reception, they were full of apprehension and anger when they beheld the gradual enclosure of their lands, the destruction of their forests, and the conversion of their game covers into cultivated fields.

The possession of land was highly esteemed by them, and formed, indeed, the basis of their tribal system, for the soil was common property. An individual might occupy a strip of ground, but the tribe alone could dispose of it. From the very outset, this peculiar tenure of land led to misunderstandings and quarrels between the natives and settlers. The natives were quite willing to receive the gifts of the new comers; but they never imagined that, in accepting them, they were abandoning their hereditary estates: they supposed that the English were merely purchasing their friendship, and the right of encamping in the country. On the other hand, the settlers held that as they had purchased the land by a formal agreement in the English fashion, it was legally their property. Hone Heke (or, as he was commonly called by the English, Johnny Hekey), an ambitious and daring chief, roused his countrymen against what he termed the aggressions of the white men. He pointed out to them that their blankets were in tatters, that their tobacco was all consumed, that their axes were blunted with use, and that, while the English gave them goods which lasted only for a brief time, they claimed for themselves the permanent possession of the land. To the British flag waving over the settlements the natives attached a superstitious character, believing that it was not merely the emblem, but the source of our power. Accordingly, they resolved to destroy it. In March

1845, Heke led a band of natives against Korarareka, the oldest settlement. The sloop-of-war, and a small detachment of troops which garrisoned the station, were overpowered, the flag-staff was cut down, and the military block-house captured. The town was then pillaged, and afterwards given to the flames. Most of the inhabitants sought shelter on board ship. Several lives were lost, and a great amount of property was destroyed. A three years' war, with varying fortunes, followed. Peace was proclaimed in February 1848. In 1860-1, 1863-4, and 1867-9, similar wars, arising from similar causes, disturbed the peaceful industry of the colony. Amicable relations seem now to be permanently established between the majority of natives and settlers.

The progress of New Zealand has of late years been very rapid. Almost within a quarter of a century, it was regarded as a country in the lowest and most debased condition, peopled by savages who were perpetually at war with each other, and who, when they subdued a foe, picked his bones at a cannibal feast. It is now a flourishing British colony. A white population of more than eighty thousand is distributed among seven settlements. Auckland, the metropolis, derives a handsome revenue from the forests of giant Kauri trees which surround it, and from the shipping which frequents its harbour. Wellington enjoys a magnificent harbour, and produces a considerable quantity of wheat and wool. Taranaki (or New Plymouth) is a robust, hearty village, in the midst of fields dotted with cattle, or waving with yellow corn. Its beauty and fertility have gained for it the attractive name of the garden of New Zealand. Canterbury thrives on its vast pastoral plains; and Otago combines farming and stock breeding. Hanke Bay, an offshoot of Wellington, is also agricultural. Nelson draws its riches from the bowels of the earth, in coal and copper. The gold-fields of Otago, however, for the time eclipse the less dazzling mineral wealth of Nelson. It has long been known that there is gold in New Zealand, but it was supposed that it did not exist in a sufficient quantity to render the working profitable. Gold was discovered some years ago at Coromandel Bay, in the north, and at Massacre Bay, in the province of Nelson; but in the former case the deposit was quickly exhausted; and in the latter, although the diggers have continued at work, their profits have been trifling. A German professor, named Hofstetter, who travelled through New Zealand two years ago, expressed his opinion that that country presented all the features of a rich gold region. Since the summer of 1861, several valuable discoveries have confirmed that opinion; and the gold-fields of Otago now form the resort of thousands of diggers. The chief deposits are found at Tuapeka, about thirty miles from Tokomairio, in a series of galleries which lie between the snow-capped Lammermoor hills and the dark, frowning Tapuanook mountain range. The progress of the colony is illustrated by the fact, that within seven years the aggregate of live stock of all kinds has increased six-fold, the land under crop five-fold, and the land fenced nearly eight-fold, while the European population has been more than doubled.

Captain Cook estimated the native population of New Zealand at three hundred thousand, and it is now only seventy thousand. Although diminished in number, the natives have shared in the general advancement. No authenticated case of cannibalism has occurred since 1844. The repugnance of the New Zealanders to systematic labour has been overcome, and they now devote themselves earnestly to industrial pursuits. A tatooed chief may now be seen, in shirt and trousers, between the handles of a plough. The natives build mills, cultivate land, rear cattle, fatten pigs, and know their weight to a pound, and their value to a penny. They are famed as horse-breakers, and almost monopolize the coasting trade of the islands.* Since 1815, missionary work has been carried on with eminent zeal and enthusiasm, but at first with slight success. The result of twenty years' labour was the conversion of only a handful of natives; but of late years Christianity has become almost universal. In all parts of the country chapels

* In 1859 the native population of the Bay of Islands was 8000. They had 9000 acres under cultivation, owned about 1000 horses, had 200 head of cattle, and 5000 pigs. They had built 4 mills, and possessed 96 ploughs, owned 43 coasting vessels, averaging 20 tons each, and 900 canoes. In the same year they supplied to English traders no less than 46,000 bushels of wheat, of the value of £13,000.

have been erected. In almost every native village the bell—sometimes an old musket barrel struck with a nail—summons the people to prayer; and the chanting of hymns often breaks the silence of the forest. In Bishop Selwyn the colony possesses a noble specimen of the Christian missionary. He steers his little ship from one group of islands to another, making a wide circuit of visits every year, and exposing himself to innumerable perils, from which he is preserved, as the natives believe, by a special grace. He thinks nothing of swimming across a river when there is no ford. He can climb the hills more readily, and walk further and faster, even than the natives; and they reverence the physical energy which is combined with so much learning and benevolence. On his tours he lodges in the native huts, and thus wins the confidence of the inmates. When he finds a promising youth, he carries him off to be educated and trained. The parents know that the good bishop will take care of their son, and that he is sincerely anxious for their welfare. Thus a bond of affectionate union is created between the New Zealander and the Englishman, which cannot fail to insure the happiness and prosperity of the colony.

The Cape and South Africa.

I.—THE BOERS.
II.—THE FALSE PROPHET OF THE KAFFIRS.

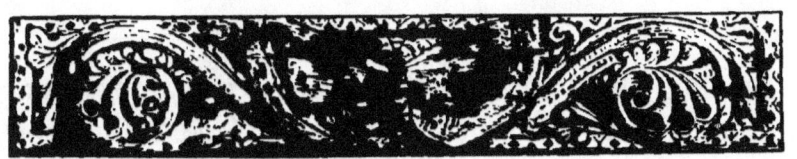

The Cape and South Africa.

I.—THE BOERS.

ORIGINALLY founded by the Dutch in 1652, the colony of the Cape of Good Hope was captured by the English in 1795, was subsequently restored to the Dutch, and was finally recovered by the English in 1815. At that period the bulk of the inhabitants were Dutchmen, or Boers; which is the Dutch word for "peasant," or "farmer." Stock breeding was the almost universal pursuit, and as the number of settlers increased, and as their flocks and herds multiplied, they naturally pushed further into the interior. As they advanced the natives had to give place. The original inhabitants of the extreme southern part of Africa were the Hottentots. These are a slothful and unwarlike race, hating toil of any kind, averse to cleanliness, but lively, cheerful, and good-humoured. Of a soft, yielding disposition, and weakened still further by being broken up into independent tribes, the Hottentots could offer no effectual resistance to the encroachments of the Dutch.

Driving their cattle before them, they were continually wandering further from the Cape. But their misfortunes did not end here. They were placed, as it were, between two fires. At first, as the Boers "trekked" inland, the Kosa Kaffirs descending from the north-east moved southwards. Between these two invaders the poor helpless Hottentots were gradually squeezed out of their land, and lived merely by sufferance on the soil which they had formerly called their own. The Kaffirs and the Boers were now face to face, and the latter found that they had to deal with a people very different from the Hottentots. Of a stalwart and commanding form, expert in war, bold, crafty, and intelligent, the Kaffir (who is supposed, from various customs peculiar to the Jews which he practises, to be a descendant of Ishmael) was able to hold his ground against the white man. For a time the Boers were thus brought to a stand-still; but at length, pricked by the necessity of providing fresh pastures for their rapidly increasing herds, some of the more daring settlers pushed across Sandy River, and established their outposts in the fields of the Kaffirs. Seeing that the Boers made so free with their land, the Kaffirs thought they were entitled to some of the fat kine of the usurpers. This the phlegmatic Dutchmen resented, and reprisals on the one hand, and fresh raids on the other, became the order of the day. Once, it is said, in a fit of exasperation, the Boers, having invited the Amandonka, an especially energetic tribe of cattle-lifters, to a friendly conference, shot them down wholesale while they were collecting beads and toys thrown down before them. But, as a rule, the settlers were too much men of business, and too much in want of labour, to sacrifice valuable property to mere hatred. They usually enslaved any Kaffirs who fell into their hands; and as the natives were yearly at war among themselves, they occasionally got a good bargain of prisoners from a victorious chief. In this way they collected troops of slaves, who did good service on the wide stock farms. When the English acquired authority in the colony in 1815, they abolished slavery. The Boers, in a rage, retired beyond the frontier. A large body of them, with a thousand waggons, and innumerable sheep and cattle, moved in successive divisions beyond the Drackenberg Mountains, and settled in the fertile district of Natal. There they established an independent government; which, of course, we refused to recognise. In a fit of resentment, they endeavoured to incite some of the native tribes to assail us. Upon this being discovered, they were attacked and overcome by a British force. The few who remained in Natal acknowledged the British sway; but the most of them shook every atom of British dust off their feet, and established themselves as a republic, to the north of the Val River, on land to which we laid no claim. There, to this day, they remain. Their hatred of England is said to be still lively :—" A Trans-Val Boer names the worst horse in his team 'England,' and always belabours and abuses it more than any other." There is, however, a number of Boers within our territory, and it must in justice be owned that they possess many estimable qualities. They are a sober, frugal, hard-working people, and generally thrive. They cling stubbornly to old habits and prejudices. They despise the coloured man as heartily as when their ancestors fleeing from persecution in Europe first settled at the Cape. They use primitive, old ploughs, which twelve stout oxen find it a tough job to draw. They know nothing of a flail, and set oxen to tread out their corn, in the old Jewish fashion. " In person," says Mr. Cole, " they are the finest men in the colony, and their strength is gigantic. They marry young, and have generally large families. To the second and third generation they live at the same homestead, building an additional hut for each newly-wedded couple. They are a very religious people, and observe the Sabbath with the greatest decorum, however far they may be situated from church or chapel. Four times a year the sacrament is administered in every Dutch church in the colony. And then from far and wide the waggons pour into the towns, bringing families who have travelled even one hundred and fifty miles to partake of the Lord's Supper."

The Boers confine themselves almost exclusively to a pastoral life, leaving trade to the British settlers. When we took possession of the Cape in 1815, the Great Fish River, which flowed between the lands of the settlers and the wild bush in which the Kaffirs lived, was a very troublesome frontier. After an inglorious and unprofitable contest with the natives, arising out of some of their cattle-stealing expeditions, our government, dissatisfied with the Boers, planted a number of Englishmen and Scotchmen along the river. These soon fell to trading with the Kaffirs, and in spite of the discouragement of the government, a flourishing commerce sprung up. The mission of the trader in Africa is full of excitement and adventure. He collects a quantity of coarse cloth, smart Manchester printed calicoes, blankets, beads, brass curtain-rings, (which serve as armlets), wide-awake hats, and snuff, for the natives; and also blankets, clothes, and provisions for the Boers. Packing these miscellaneous stores in a couple of long bulky Cape waggons, each driven by twelve or fourteen oxen, and accompanied by a couple of lazy, roguish Hottentots, the trader starts for the interior. As his oxen have to find their food by the way-side, he moves at the rate of not more than twenty or twenty-five miles a day. Towards dusk he relieves the cattle from the yoke, and encamps under the dark, cloudless blue of the African night; and as he dozes off to sleep, hears, perhaps, by way of lullaby, the howl of the prowling hyena, the majestic roar of the lion, or the shrill trumpet of the elephant. When he reaches the solitary homestead of a Boer he halts for a day or two. The Boer is a cautious man, and likes to examine the goods carefully before he buys them. Besides, the trader full of news about the bustling world, is too great a luxury to be soon parted with. At first the Boer invariably declares that he is in want of nothing whatever, and it is not till the second or third day that he consents to purchase any goods. It is, however, with the natives that the trader drives the most profitable trade. They pay not in money, but in kind,—in elephant tusks, ostrich feathers, and the skins and horns of wild beasts. With these he reloads his waggons, and, retracing his steps, finds himself again at home, after an absence of six or eight months.

The natives do not monopolize the supply of the spoils of the chase. Many European hunters, chiefly British, wage fierce war upon the beasts of the African bush, and accumulate immense quantities of ivory and skins. One daring sportsman in three months killed seventy elephants, the tusks of which weighed three thousand pounds. In the same period the Boers sometimes collect as much as thirty tons of ivory in a single district. Between the rifles of the whites and the lassos or traps of the blacks, the wild animals are gradually disappearing in Southern

Africa. The lion, hippopotamus, rhinoceros, giraffe, and other large "game," have all retreated deep into the interior. It is supposed that there is not now a single lion within the limits of Cape Colony; but it is still met with in the thinly settled parts of Natal and in the Trans-Val country.

II.—THE FALSE PROPHET OF THE KAFFIRS.

Details of the miserable wars between natives and settlers, of Kaffir strategy and cunning, of dogged Saxon courage and perseverance bestowed on an inglorious cause of treacherous ambuscades and savage reprisals, occupy a large portion of the history of African colonization. Into such details we need not enter. It is enough to say, that between 1806 and 1853 we engaged in many campaigns against the Kaffirs, with little honour and much loss. After the defeat of the Kaffirs in 1846, the region now known as British Kaffraria, whence used to descend those hordes which devastated our frontier, was formed into a colonial province. A considerable number of the natives, however, continued to reside in it. Their kraals, or villages, dotted the ridges and slopes between which flowed the streams of the country. The pastures, being very rich, supported large flocks and herds; and the district was, therefore, densely peopled, several kraals being always in sight of each other. The military organization of the Kaffirs was very complete. They could at any moment bring into the field at least sixteen hundred men, armed with spears and fire-arms, who owned ready obedience to their chiefs, and were well officered. For the greater part of the year the warriors lounged idly about the villages, and they rarely or never wandered from place to place. A small stream divides British Kaffraria from Kaffraria proper, where dwelt a yet more numerous Kaffir population, who could join forces with their countrymen in an instant. Sir George Grey, the governor of the Cape, saw in these facts good reason for apprehension as to the safety of the colony from a destructive attack by the Kaffirs. It was known that they were in a restless, mischievous mood, that they outnumbered the Europeans, and formed a compact body disciplined in war; while, on the other hand, the colonists were men of peace, and were scattered over a large extent of country. The governor was concentrating all his resources, and urging the mother country to send out more troops, when an incident happened which seemingly threatened to destroy the British colony, but in the most singular manner proved its deliverance.

A prophet appeared among the Kaffirs, who declared that on an appointed day, when the sun rose it would wander for a time in the heavens, and set again in the east. Immediately thereafter a hurricane would begin to blow, which would sweep from the face of the earth all who had not believed in the prophecy, and obeyed the mandates of the prophet, whether Kaffirs or Europeans. Then the ancestors of the Kaffirs would arise from the dead, with all manner of rich goods, and countless herds of cattle, nobler in proportions, sleeker in the coats, and fatter in the ribs than those which had before browsed upon the pastures of Kaffraria. Those bounties would be lavished on the faithful, who, thenceforth restored to youth and endowed with unfading strength and beauty, were to have the whole land to themselves. In order to share in the blessings of this new dispensation, however, the Kaffirs (so said the prophet) must destroy all their corn and cattle, and refrain from cultivating the ground until the miracle had been performed. From this sweeping condemnation of property, horses, arms, and ammunition were specially exempted; and there appears but little doubt that the whole affair was a conspiracy between a number of the leading chiefs and high priests to reduce the people to destitution and desperation, in the hope that they would then wage a ruthless and exterminating war against the white men. At the instigation, and in some cases under the menaces, of their leaders, a great many of the people slaughtered all their cattle and burned their grain. They then repaired the roofs and pillars of their huts, in order that they might be strong enough to withstand the anticipated hurricane. On the eve of the day named by the prophet (the 18th March 1857), they shut themselves up within their huts to await the fearful events of the morrow. Through chinks in the wall the rays of the morning sun streaked the gloom of their squalid dwellings, but they were afraid to look out to see whether the great luminary was pursuing its ordinary course, or staggering through the heavens. Morning wore to noon without a sign of an eclipse, and without the most distant rumble of a hurricane. Night fell, and still the prophecy was unfulfilled. Next morning the unhappy and deluded Kaffirs came out of their houses, downcast, destitute, and desperate. Many were real and earnest believers in the prophet, and had destroyed every ox and sheep, and every grain of corn which they possessed. Some of the great chiefs, who used to count their hundreds of head of cattle, had now not a single one left. There were others who encouraged the movement in the hope that it would lead to war and tumult, and who, sacrificing only a portion of their stock, confided the rest to the keeping of friends in a remote district. About a third of the population, turning a deaf ear to the commands of the prophet, preserved their herds and flocks, and tilled their lands as usual. Soon two parties divided the land, the believers and the unbelievers,—those who had destroyed their property, and those who had retained it. The country was covered with crowds of women and children digging up wild roots for food. Several chiefs committed suicide in despair. Their subjects were heart-broken and famishing. Two-thirds of the entire people disappeared from British Kaffraria in the first seven months of 1857. The population of Kaffraria proper underwent even greater diminution. Upwards of thirty thousand Kaffirs entered service in the colony, some thousands took refuge with other tribes, and some thousands perished from want.

The military organization of the Kaffirs was thus broken up, and the influence of their chiefs was in a large measure dissipated. Their herds and flocks being gone, they had to become inured to systematic labour in the fields or in the towns. It is not improbable that they will now form an important element in the industrial life, and contribute largely to the prosperity, of the colony. At any rate, the constant menace of a native war, which formerly hung like a dark storm-cloud over the settlements, has passed away.

The extended exploration of Africa, and the important experiments which have lately been made to test its productive resources, raise well-founded hopes of a magnificent future for this great continent. Till just the other day the vast interior remained, as it had been for centuries, a hidden land, from the investigation of which travellers were deterred by miasma on the sea-board, and the wide tracts of sandy desert which stretched further inland. If our modern geographers did not in their maps depict the heart of Africa as peopled with strange and fabulous monsters, it was certainly not because they knew anything more than those of old regarding its soil, climate, or inhabitants. Within the last few years, however, important discoveries have been made. Livingstone has tracked the great river Zambesi across the continent from its mouths on the east coast to Loanda on the west. Burton and Speke succeeded, after a journey of seven and a half months, in finding, at a direct distance of 540 miles from the coast, opposite to Zanzibar, a great internal lake called Tanganyika, 250 miles in length, and with a mean breadth of 20 miles, covering about 5000 square miles with its waters. In addition to this, Speke and Grant discovered the existence of another lake —that of Nyanza, north-east of Tanganyika—the area of which is supposed to be even more considerable. Further: Petherick, following the course of the Nile, has reached the Mountains of the Moon, and nearly connected his route with that of Speke and Burton. It almost takes one's breath away to hear the grand speculation which the results of these journeys have suggested,—that there is a connection between the Nile and Lake Nyanza, so that vessels of light burden may be able to pass from the Mediterranean into the very core of Africa, and the flags of all nations float on the blue waters of the great inland sea. Yet the idea is by no means so wild as at first it seems, and is supported by eminent scientific authorities. Krapf in eastern, and Barth in northern Africa have also added to our materials for mapping out this enormous region, which has been justly designated the continent of the future.

In the present state of our cotton supply, the proved capacity of Africa to produce that valuable article is of great consequence; and is perhaps more likely than anything else to stimulate the development of its resources. Africa bids fair to become a market in which we shall be able not only to procure the raw material, but dispose of the manufactured goods. To the natives, Dr. Livingstone says, our cotton mills are fairy dreams. They cannot conceive how cloth of such fine and delicate texture can be the work of machinery, or even of mortals. "How can irons spin, and weave, and print so beautifully?" they ask; and an attempt to explain the process is usually followed by the exclamation, "Truly ye are gods!"

Pitcairn's Island.

Pitcairn's Island.

ON the 27th April 1789, the crew of His Majesty's ship *Bounty*, then cruising in the neighbourhood of the Friendly Islands, broke out into open mutiny. In the dead of night a number of the sailors entered the cabin of the captain, Bligh, bound his hands behind his back, and carrying him on deck, compelled him, with eighteen others who would not join the conspiracy, to descend into one of the ship's boats. A small quantity of bread and pork, with two or three bottles of wine and spirits, were thrown after them; and thus supplied, the little craft set forth on its perilous voyage over the broad waters. Driven by the hostility of the natives from one of the Friendly Islands, where they sought to land, the unhappy victims spent forty-eight days and nights on the ocean, exposed to the rigour of the elements, reduced during the latter part of their voyage to a quarter of a pint of cocoa-nut milk, as much bread as would weigh down a pistol bullet, an ounce of pork once a day, and a tea-spoonful of water every eight hours.

At the end of that period of suffering they reached the Dutch station at Coupang, whence they procured a passage home. When the news of this atrocious outrage reached England, the frigate *Pandora* was at once despatched to capture the mutineers. Fourteen of them were seized at Tahiti, where the graves of two or three others were pointed out. Of the remaining nine no trace whatever could be discovered, and the *Pandora* sailed away under the belief that they had perished at sea or under the clubs of the savages. The frigate was wrecked on its homeward voyage. Four of the prisoners were drowned; the remaining ten were conveyed to England, where four were acquitted, three pardoned, and three hung at the yard-arm.

Twenty-five years rolled by, and the occurrence had almost faded from the recollection of men. In 1814, a couple of English men-of-war anchored off a pleasant island in the Pacific, about twelve hundred miles from Tahiti. Situated just beyond the tropics, having a rich and luxuriant vegetation, without the unhealthiness of a too luxuriant fertility, this green little speck on the bosom of the ocean tempted the sailors, weary of hard biscuits and salt pork, to visit it in search of fresh fruits and vegetables. Their surprise may be imagined, when, on approaching the shore, they beheld huts peeping forth among the groves. A couple of the islanders were observed to run down to the beach with canoes on their backs, which they launched and quickly paddled towards the big ships. The sailors could hardly believe their ears when they heard one of the canoe-men call out, in good English, " Come, look alive there, and throw us a rope." When the visitors appeared on deck, they were seen to be two strapping, well-made young fellows, with handsome features of an English cast, but somewhat darker in complexion than the ordinary Anglo-Saxon tint. A strip of cotton round their middle, and a broad-brimmed straw hat adorned with black feathers, composed their entire costume, so that their muscular frames and imposing proportions (each being about six feet in height) were displayed to full advantage. Sir Thomas Staines, the captain, invited them to his table, and was much touched to observe that before a morsel passed their lips, they clasped their hands, bent their heads, and reverently said grace.

The wonder of the English crews reached its climax when, on landing, they were greeted by an Englishman of venerable appearance, who disclosed himself as the sole survivor of the nine mutineers of the *Bounty* who had evaded the search of the *Pandora*, and were supposed to have died. His story was listened to with breathless interest. Twice repulsed by the natives from Tahiti, the mutineers, at the instigation of Fletcher Christian, their leader, steered for Pitcairn's Island, of which he had read in a volume of voyages which he picked up in the captain's cabin. Scarcely five miles in circumference, it looked like a great rock rising from the waves. Lofty, precipitous cliffs rose from the sea on every side save one, where there was a narrow fringe of beach leading to a steep ascent, shaded with cocoa, bread-fruit, and banana trees. Twenty-eight persons disembarked from the *Bounty*. There were nine mutineers (one having died), each with a woman of Tahiti, whom he had taken to wife; and six natives of the same island, of whom three were married, and one had an infant. Grotesque representations of the sun, moon, and other objects of idolatry, graven on the rocks, several spear-heads made of flint, and a few ghastly skulls which were strewed about, proved that the island had been inhabited before they arrived; but they found no trace of any other living being than themselves. Almost one of their first acts was to destroy the *Bounty*. Thus they cut off from themselves all means of escape from their island prison. Dissolute and passionate men, destitute of moral principle and self-control, they soon showed that they had not got rid of one authority in order to subject themselves to another. Christian tried to maintain some sort of order amongst them, and for a short time succeeded. Soon the Englishmen and the Tahitians came to blows, and blood was shed on both sides. The blacks conspired to murder the whites; but the wives of the latter discovered the plot on the eve of its execution. The result of such feuds it is not difficult to conceive. In less than a year Christian and four of his companions were massacred by the Tahitians; who, in turn, all died violent deaths before the same year closed. One of the Englishmen, with perverse ingenuity, converted an old copper kettle, which he had brought from the ship, into an alembic, and distilled an intoxicating liquor from the root of a plant which grew on the island. This introduced a new element of misery among the unhappy settlers. The man who had invented the liquor, in a fit of *delirium tremens* flung himself from a high cliff into the sea. The desperate Englishmen having no Indians to abuse, quarrelled with each other, and several fatal conflicts ensued. Up to the time when the English ships discovered the colony, only one of the mutineers had died a natural death, and John Adams was the sole survivor. Although only fifty years of age, the terrible scenes in which he had taken part, and the anxiety and remorse which they had caused, had wrinkled his brow and blanched his hair, so that he seemed quite an old man. By the widows and children of his old companions he was looked up to as a patriarch. He had rescued from the *Bounty* a Bible and a book of prayers, in the perusal of which he found sweet consolation in the midst of his misery. He had devoted himself zealously to the education of the young, read to them daily portions of the Holy Writ, and taught their tongues to lisp a prayer. He also maintained order in the island, and was always resorted to for advice in difficulties or as an umpire in disputes. Notwithstanding his reformed life, it was a long time before Adams ceased to be disturbed by a dread of retribution for his share in the mutiny. Once or twice a vessel had approached the island, and he and the other Englishmen had hid themselves in caves, until their sails no longer specked the waters. When Sir Thomas Staines arrived, however, Adams conquered his first impulse to conceal himself, and came down to the beach to welcome his countrymen.

A glimpse of the condition of this singular colony, when first discovered, is given by an officer of one of the men-of-war:—

"Their native modesty," he says, "assisted by a proper sense of religion and morality, instilled into their youthful minds by John Adams, had hitherto preserved these interesting people pure and uncorrupted. They all labour, while young, in the cultivation of the ground; and when possessed of a sufficient quantity of cleared land and of stock to maintain a family, they are allowed to marry, but always with the consent of Adams. The greatest harmony prevails in this little society; their only quarrels, and these rarely happen, being, according to their own expression, ' quarrels of the mouth.' They are honest in their dealings, which consist of bartering different articles for mutual accommodation.

Their habitations are extremely neat. The little village of Pitcairn forms a pretty square, the houses at the upper end being occupied by the patriarch Adams and his family. On the opposite side is the dwelling of Thursday October Christian; and in the centre is a smooth verdant lawn on which the poultry are let loose, fenced in so as to prevent the intrusion of the domestic quadrupeds. Everything appeared to be done according to a settled plan. In the houses they had a good deal of decent furniture, consisting of beds laid upon bedsteads, with neat covering; they had also tables, and large chests to contain their valuables and clothing, which is made from the bark of a tree chiefly by the elder women. Adams's house consisted of two rooms, and the windows had shutters which were closed at night. The younger women are, along with the young men, employed, under the direction of Adams, in the culture of the ground, which produced cocoa-nuts, bananas, the bread-fruit tree, yams, sweet potatoes, and turnips. They have also plenty of hogs and goats. The woods abound with a species of wild hog, and the coasts of the island with several kinds of good fish. Their agricultural implements are made by themselves from the iron supplied by the *Bounty*, which, with great labour, they beat out into spades, hatchets, &c. The old man kept a journal, in which was entered the nature and quantity of work performed by each family, what each had received, and what was due on account. Besides private property, there was a general stock, out of which articles were issued on credit to the several members of the community; and, for mutual accommodation, exchanges of one kind of provision for another were very frequent,—as, salt for fresh provisions, vegetables and fruit for poultry, fish, &c. Also, when the stores of one family were low or wholly expended, a fresh supply was raised from another, or out of the general stock, to be repaid when circumstances were more favourable."

Once introduced to the knowledge of Europeans, the Pitcairn islanders received frequent visits from passing ships. Their primitive ideas as to dress and other matters were enlarged; and they began to exchange the produce of their little farms for articles of comfort and luxury. The young men might be seen strutting about, one in a black swallow-tailed coat, another in a shirt and trousers. Shoes and stockings were gradually introduced, and a battered beaver was occasionally donned on festivals. The sale of spirits was strictly prohibited; but tea, coffee, sugar, flour, &c., were gladly received.

In the course of years this little colony multiplied to such a degree that it outgrew its agricultural resources. As the island could no longer afford sustenance to its inhabitants, they sought a home elsewhere. In 1857 they were removed, at their own request, but at the expense of the British government, to Norfolk Island. Here in former days was located a penal settlement, of which many a tale of horror is told. Where once stood the grim barrack into which the wretched convicts used to be driven at dusk, to prey upon each other till morning, and before the grated windows of which stalked sentries who had orders to fire into any room where they heard a tumult, if at their bidding it did not at once cease—now stand the little chapel and the schools of the new colonists. A congregation of the most brutal criminals has given place to a community of the most innocent and undepraved people in the world. Thus transformed, Norfolk Island now represents the land of which the poets have had visions,—

> "Those happy shores,
> Where none contest the fields, the woods, the streams,—
> The golden age where gold disturbs no dreams."

Norfolk Island is one thousand miles from Sydney. Girdled by a coral reef, it is very difficult of approach; but when reached is found to be a place of great beauty and fertility. It consists of a series of hills curiously interwoven, crowned with magnificent groves of gigantic pine, graceful palmetto, guava, lemon, and fern trees. Yellow corn-fields wave by the side of gardens in which grow the delicate cinnamon tree, the tea and coffee shrubs, the sugar-cane, the banana, and luxuriant vines. It cannot be doubted that the good islanders have been fortunate in exchanging Pitcairn for Norfolk Island; and it is gratifying to know that their life, if not so primitive, is as peaceful and happy as in their old home. The patriarch Adams died in 1829 in his sixty-fifth year; and Mrs. Young, the last survivor of those who arrived at Pitcairn Island in the *Bounty*, died in 1850. It remains to be seen what effect more extended intercourse with the rest of the world will have on this singular community. *

* Since these pages were written, a considerable number of the settlers in Norfolk Island returned, with the consent of the British Government (1859), to the Old Home. A recent visitor to Pitcairn's Island paints it as an oceanic Arcadia.

APPENDIX.

APPENDIX.

THE following particulars will enable the reader to form a general idea of the extent and varied character of our Colonial Empire, which now comprises fifty colonies, with an aggregate area of more than five million square miles, and a population exceeding eleven millions, about seven millions of whom are of European race :—

NORTH AMERICA.

COLONY.	HOW OBTAINED.	DATE.
THE DOMINION OF CANADA	Capitulation	1760
Including—		
NOVA SCOTIA*	Settlement	1623
	Ceded to France	1667
	Restored	1713
NEW BRUNSWICK*	Separated from Nova Scotia	1784
PRINCE EDWARD'S ISLAND*	Separated from Nova Scotia	1771
NEWFOUNDLAND*	Possession taken	1583
BERMUDA	Settlement	1609
VANCOUVER'S ISLAND†	Settlement	1792
BRITISH COLUMBIA‡	Settlement	1858

WEST INDIES.

JAMAICA	Capitulation	1655
TURKS AND CAICOS ISLANDS	Separated from Bahamas	1848
HONDURAS	Treaty	1670
BAHAMAS	Settlement	1629

* United in the Dominion, 1869. † United to British Columbia.
‡ United to the Dominion, 1871.

WEST INDIES—*Continued.*

COLONY.	How Obtained.	Date.
Barbadoes	Settlement	1605
St. Vincent	Cession	1763
Grenada	Cession	1763
Tobago	Cession	1763
St. Lucia	Capitulation	1803
Antigua	Settlement	1632
Montserrat	Settlement	1632
St. Christopher	{ Settlement	1626
	Cession	1713
	Restored	1783
Nevis	{ Settlement	1628
	Restored from French	1783
Virgin Islands	Settlement	1665
Dominica	Cession	1763
British Guiana	Capitulation	1803
Trinidad	Capitulation	1797

MEDITERRANEAN AND AFRICAN POSSESSIONS.

Gibraltar	Capitulation	1704
Malta	Capitulation	1800
Fernando Po	Capitulation	1827
Cape of Good Hope	Capitulation	1806
Natal	Separated from Cape, Letters Patent	1844
St. Helena	{ Capitulated	1600
	Settlement by East India Company	1654
	Vested in Crown	1833
Sierra Leone	Settlement	1767
Gambia	Settlement	1783
Gold Coast	Settlement	1618

AUSTRALIAN COLONIES.

New South Wales	Settlement	1788
Queensland (late Moreton Bay)	Separated from New South Wales by Letters Patent	1859
Tasmania	Settlement	1803

AUSTRALIAN COLONIES—*Continued.*

COLONY.	How Obtained.	Date.
South Australia	Settlement	1834
Victoria	Separated from New South Wales	1837
Western Australia	Settlement	1829
New Zealand	Settlement (1814), and Treaty	1840
North Australia	Settlement	1865

OTHER COLONIES.

Mauritius	Capitulation	1810
Ceylon	Capitulation	1795
Hong Kong and Cowloon	Treaties	1843, 1860
Labuan	Cession	1848
Falkland Islands	Settlement	1765
Heligoland	Capitulation	1807
Penang or Prince of Wales Island	Settlement	1785
Dutch Guinea	Purchase	1871

www.ingramcontent.com/pod-product-compliance
Lightning Source LLC
Chambersburg PA
CBHW021349230426
43666CB00006B/463